Gifted and Talented Preparation Workbook
NNAT2 – Level A

A 60-question kindergarten workbook

Bee Tutored

First Edition

Copyright © 2012

Published by Juania Books,LLC
All rights reserved

No parts of this book may be reproduced in any form without permission. The scanning, uploading, distribution via the internet or any other means including information storage and retrieval systems, without the written permission of the publisher is illegal and punishable by law. Please do not participate in or encourage electronic piracy of copyrighted materials. Your support for the author's right is appreciated.

ISBN 978-0-9818047-6-7
Gifted and Talented Preparation Workbook NNAT2
Level A Kindergarten

Created by Lauren Young for Bee Tutored Test Prep Series

Printed in the United States of America
First printing 2012

Table of contents

About Bee Tutored 2
About the NNAT 2 2
Pattern Completion 5
Reasoning by Analogy 15
Serial (Matrix) Reasoning 25
Spatial Visualization 35
Answer Key 44

About Bee Tutored

As a premier tutoring boutique, Bee Tutored has offered an exceptional level of service to the families in all areas of study since 2007. We have built a reputation of excellence based on our high level of success with students of all ages and subjects. Our highly qualified tutors provide individualized instruction from the elementary level through college prep. We ensure long-term academic success by maintaining proactive communication between students, parents, and school administrators.

About the NNAT 2

What is the NNAT 2? The NNAT2 stands for Naglieri Nonverbal Ability Test, 2nd edition. This is a 30-minute, computer-based test which offers a reliable evaluation of student's reasoning and problem-solving skills. It is currently used to gain admission into the New York City Gifted and Talented programs as well as other programs nationwide.

How is it different? The NNAT 2, which replaced the Bracken exam in 2012, is specifically designed to be culturally neutral and to eliminate test biases. Children are not required to speak, read or write when completing the exam. As indicated in the name, this test assesses nonverbal skills and is equally effective in evaluating English-speaking and non-English speaking children alike. The ability to succeed on a nonverbal assessment is believed to be a strong indicator of academic skills because it assess the same faculties that enable children to learn and synthesize new and challenging information.

How does NNAT 2 eliminate test biases? A test bias is a method of assessment that, in one way or another, gives an advantage to certain students based on their membership to a specific group. The NNAT2 is able to successfully eliminate test biases in a few ways. First, it does not require students to read, write or speak, therefore differences in primary language, culture and other important socioeconomic factors do not in any way interfere with the evaluation. Secondly, the NNAT2 does not require any prior knowledge such as reading or mathematics – everything needed to correctly answer the question is contained in the given illustrations. In this way, educational background becomes irrelevant as students are not required to identify the geometric shapes or use any other factual information. Instead they must identify different patterns and spatial relationships and determine how to complete them. In effect, the NNAT2 focuses on ability which is viewed as independent of curriculum. Finally, the method of scoring greatly reduces any age bias (see Scoring).

Which version will my child take? The NNAT2 is divided into 7 levels, and children will take the test for the level that corresponds to the grade they are entering. The levels are listed in the chart below:

GRADE	LEVEL
K	A
1	B
2	C
3 & 4	D
5 & 6	E
7, 8, & 9	F
10, 11, & 12	G

How is the NNAT2 structured? The NNAT2 is a 30-minute, computer-based test which only uses universally recognized geometric shapes. There are 48 questions, each of which is full color and in matrix, or pattern, format. The child must choose from one of 5 answers to complete the geometric sequences and is not required to read, write or speak for the entire exam.

What topics are covered on the test? Each level of the NNAT2 is comprised of 4 types of questions. These are Pattern Completion, Reasoning by Analogy, Serial Reasoning and Spatial Visualization.

Pattern Completion: These questions require the child to first determine what specific pattern is present within a rectangle and to then choose which piece in the answers completes rectangle and extends the pattern into the missing space. These questions, typically are viewed as the most simple not the NNAT2 and are more prominent in lower level tests.

Reasoning by Analogy: These questions require the perception of the logical relationship between several geometric shapes across rows and down columns. The shapes can change in one or more dimension (for example, size and shape).

Serial Reasoning: These questions require the child to first recognize a sequence of shapes (e.g., circle—square—triangle) and then to determine how the sequence changes across rows and down columns.

Spatial Visualization: These are the most difficult of the questions on the NNAT2 and require recognition of how two or more designs would look if combined. Spatial Visualization may involve rotations or intersections of shapes and are more prominent in upper levels.

How is the NNAT2 scored? A students NAI, or Naglieri Ability Index score, is rated between 50 and 150, with the mean set at 100. Therefore a score of 120 is above average and 90 is below average. The NAI is calculated by determining how many questions were answered correctly in relation to others in the age group. The NAI scoring system divides the year into four 3-month periods and students are only scored in relationship to others with birthdays in the same time brackets. By scoring the assessments only in relation to students born within 3 months of each other, the NNAT2 reduces the age bias which can result from comparing children with others at different developmental stages.

Pattern Completion

These questions are similar to an incomplete puzzle. The child will be shown a figure where one complete piece has been removed and he or she must choose which answer will correctly fit into the space. This type of question is very common on the NNAT 2 Level A test.

NNAT 2 - Pattern Completion   Bee Tutored

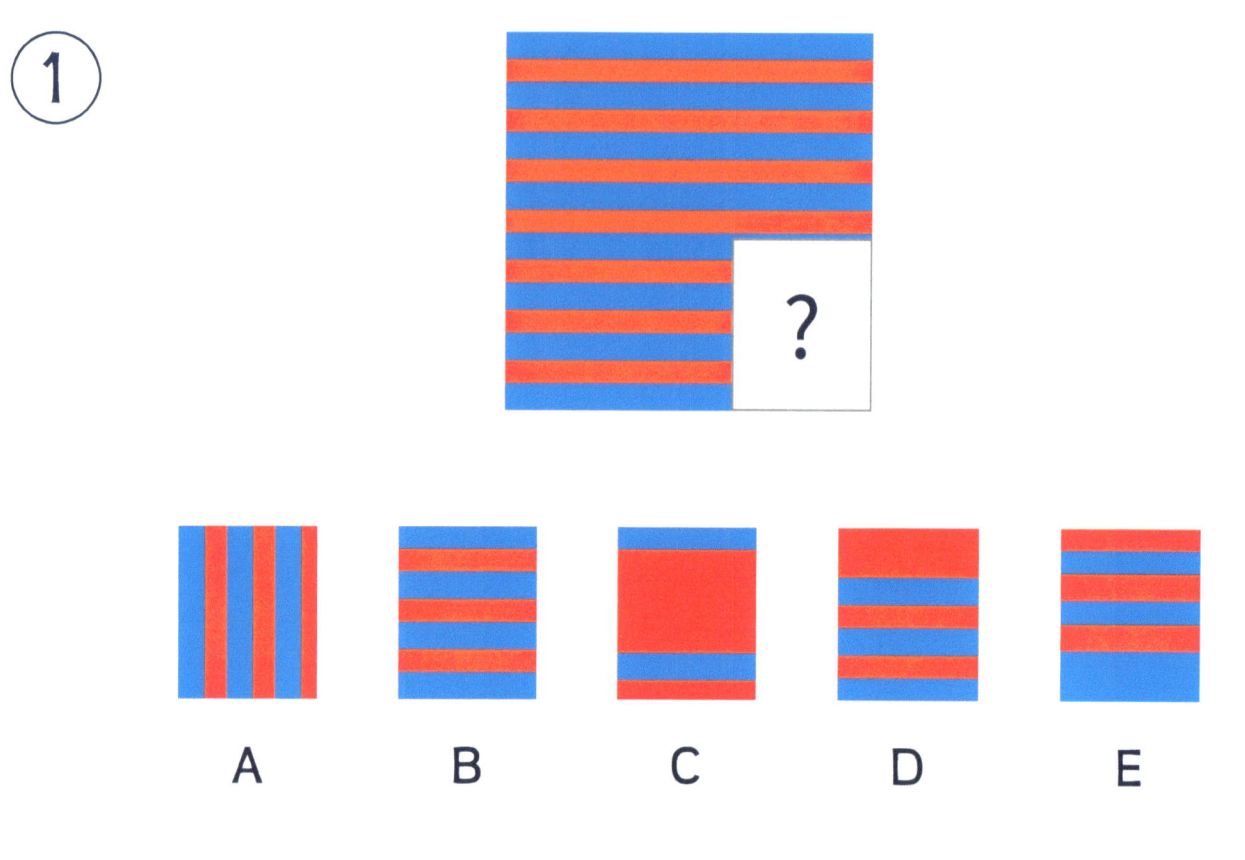

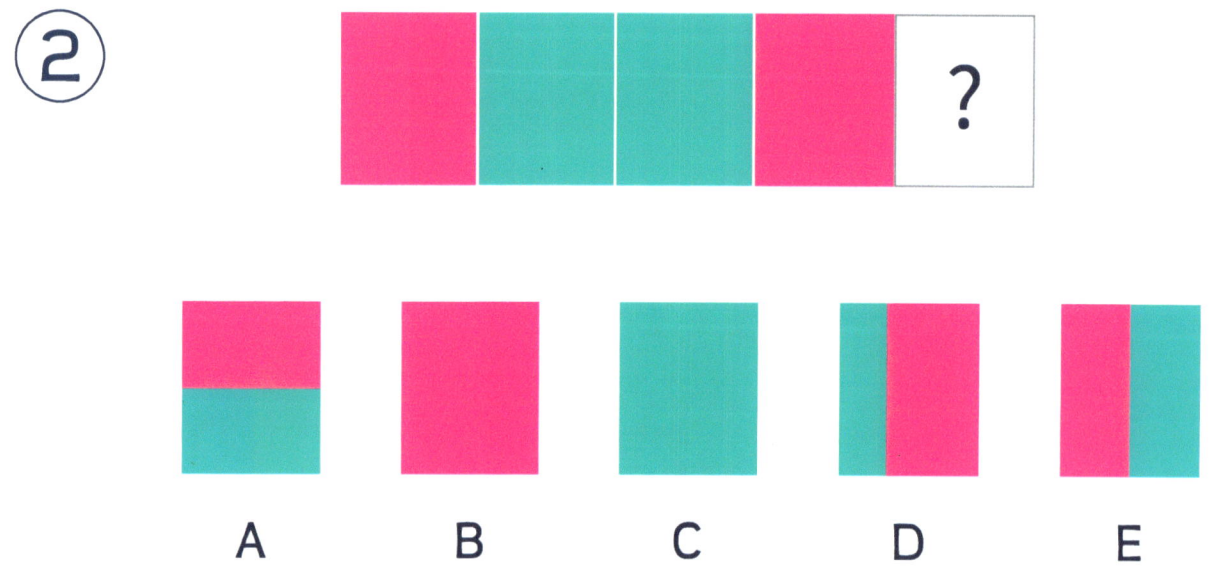

③

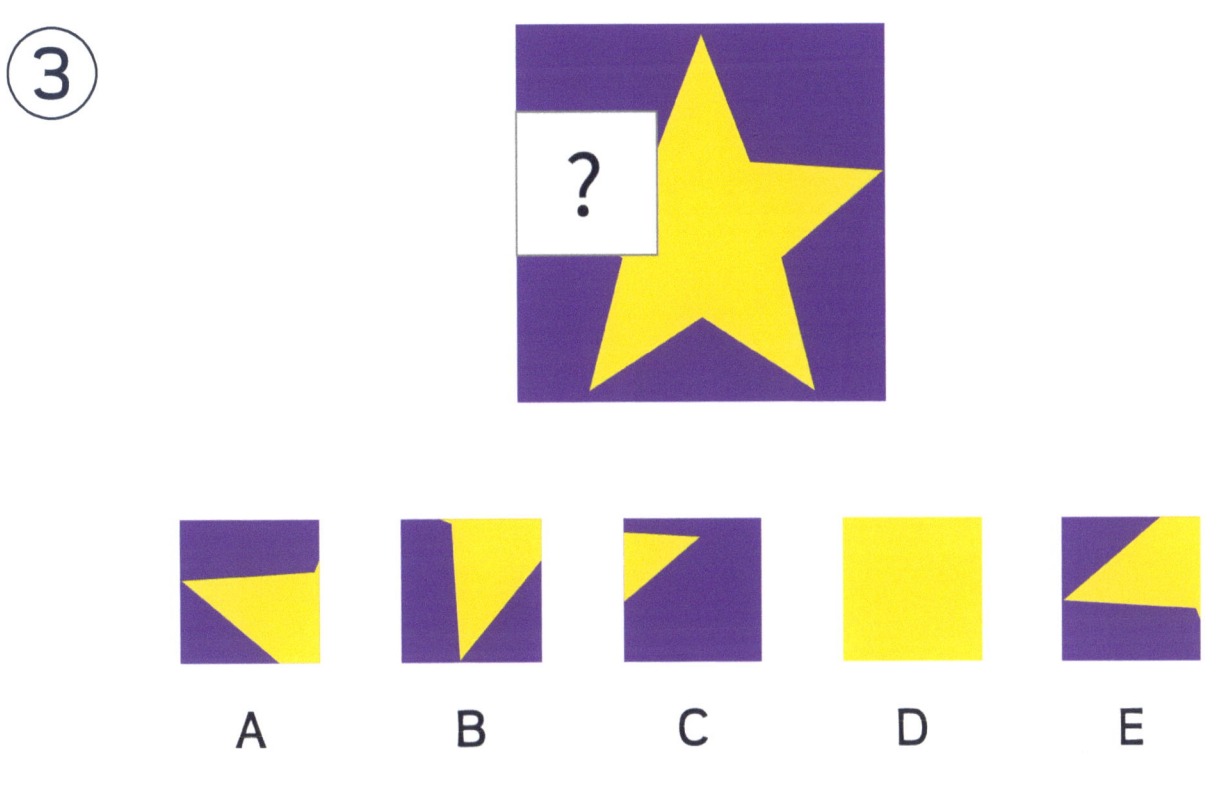

④

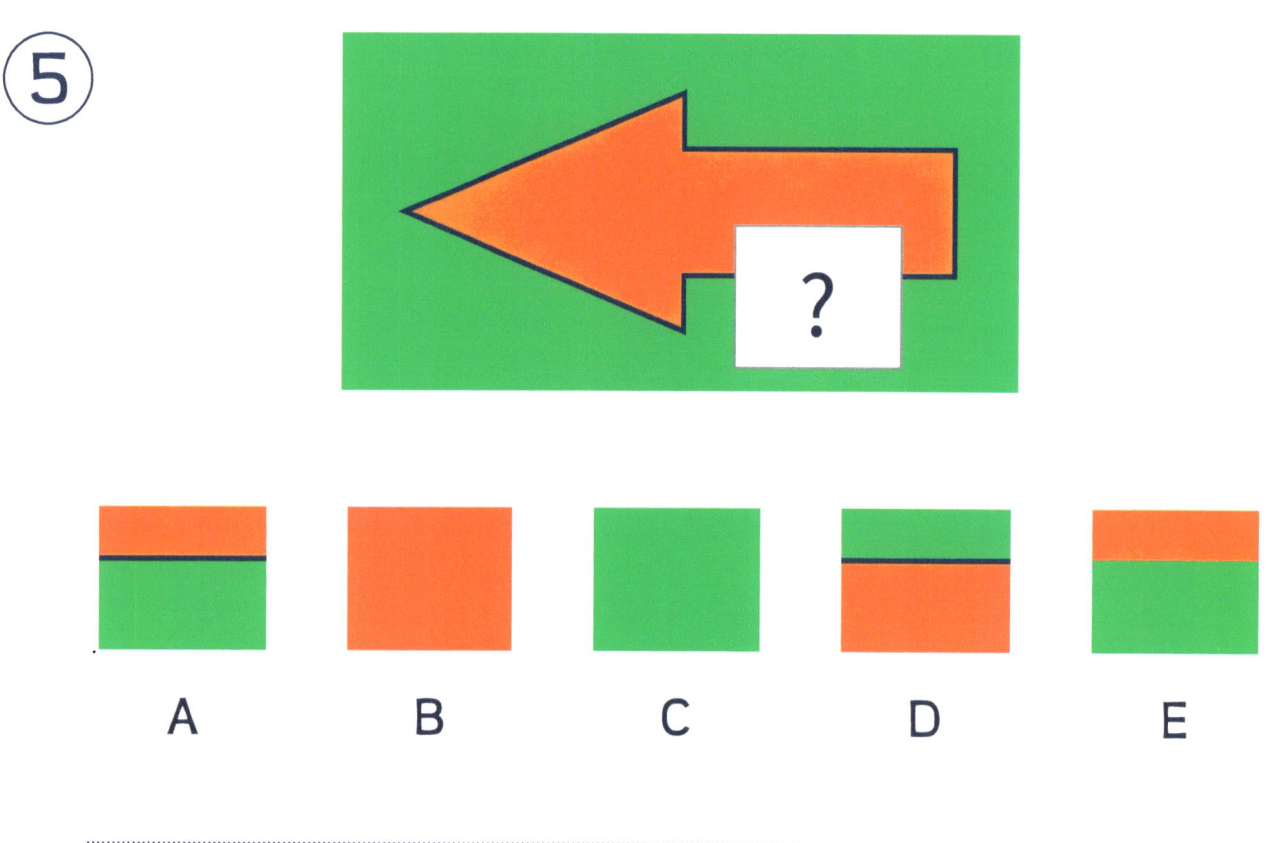

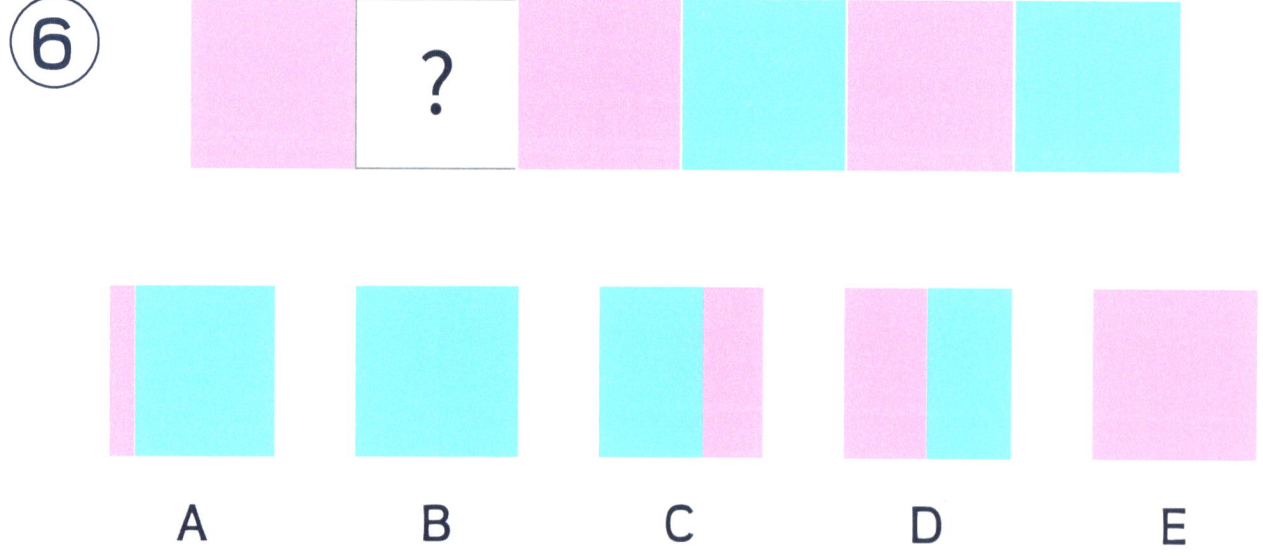

7

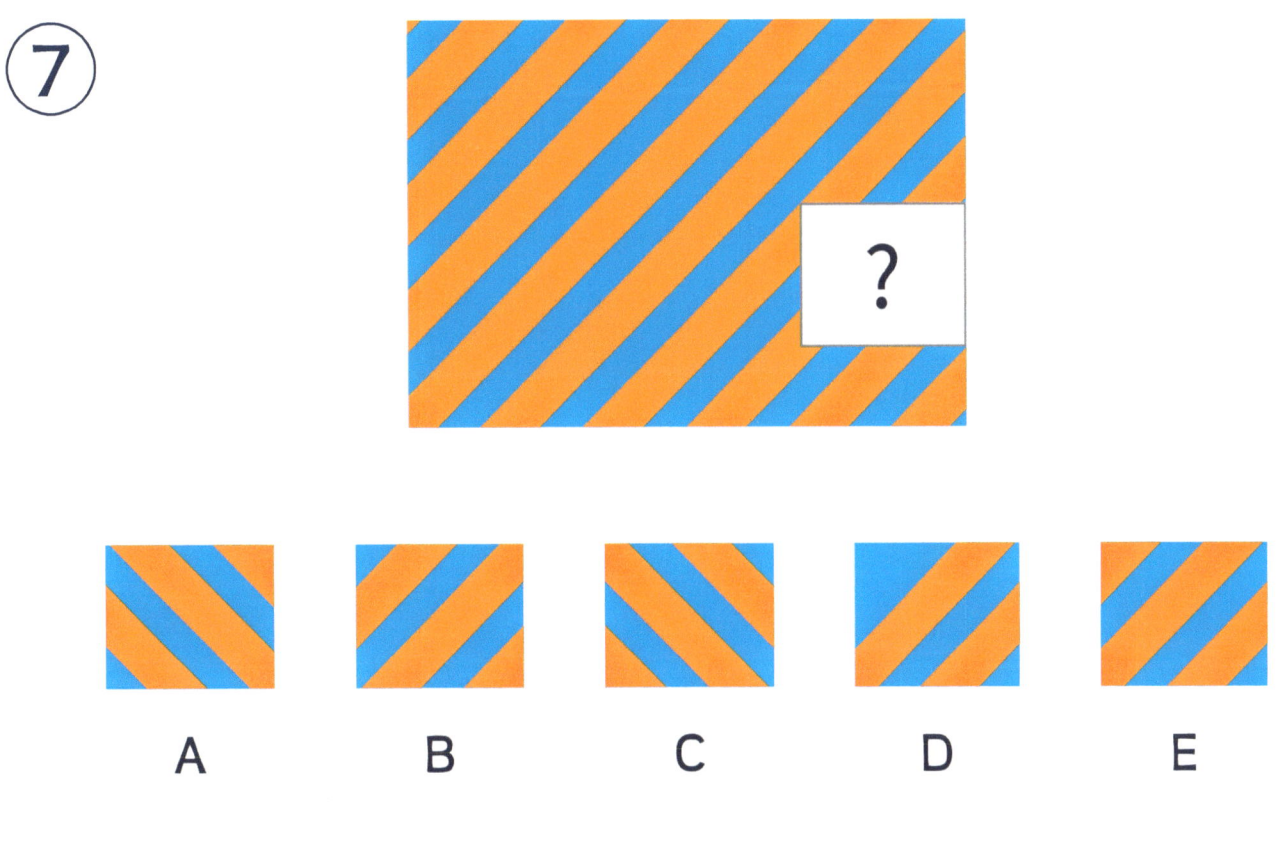

8

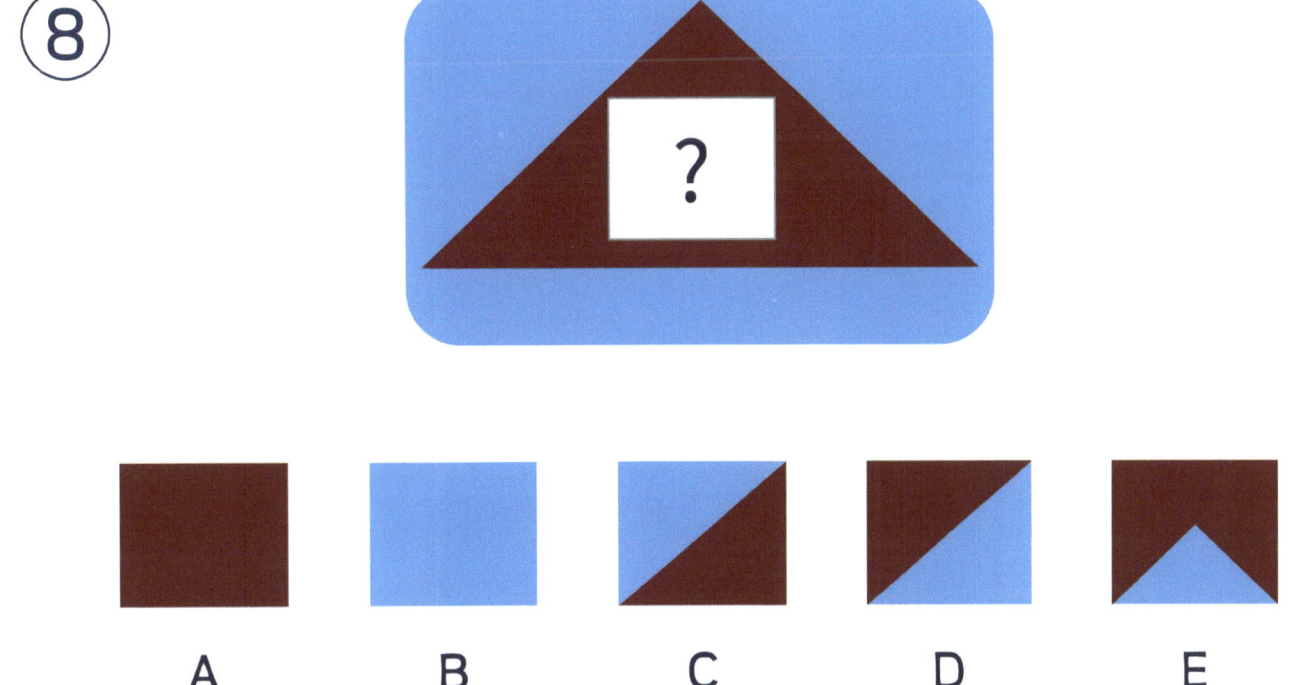

NNAT 2 - Pattern Completion　　　　　　　　　　　　　　　　　　Bee Tutored

9

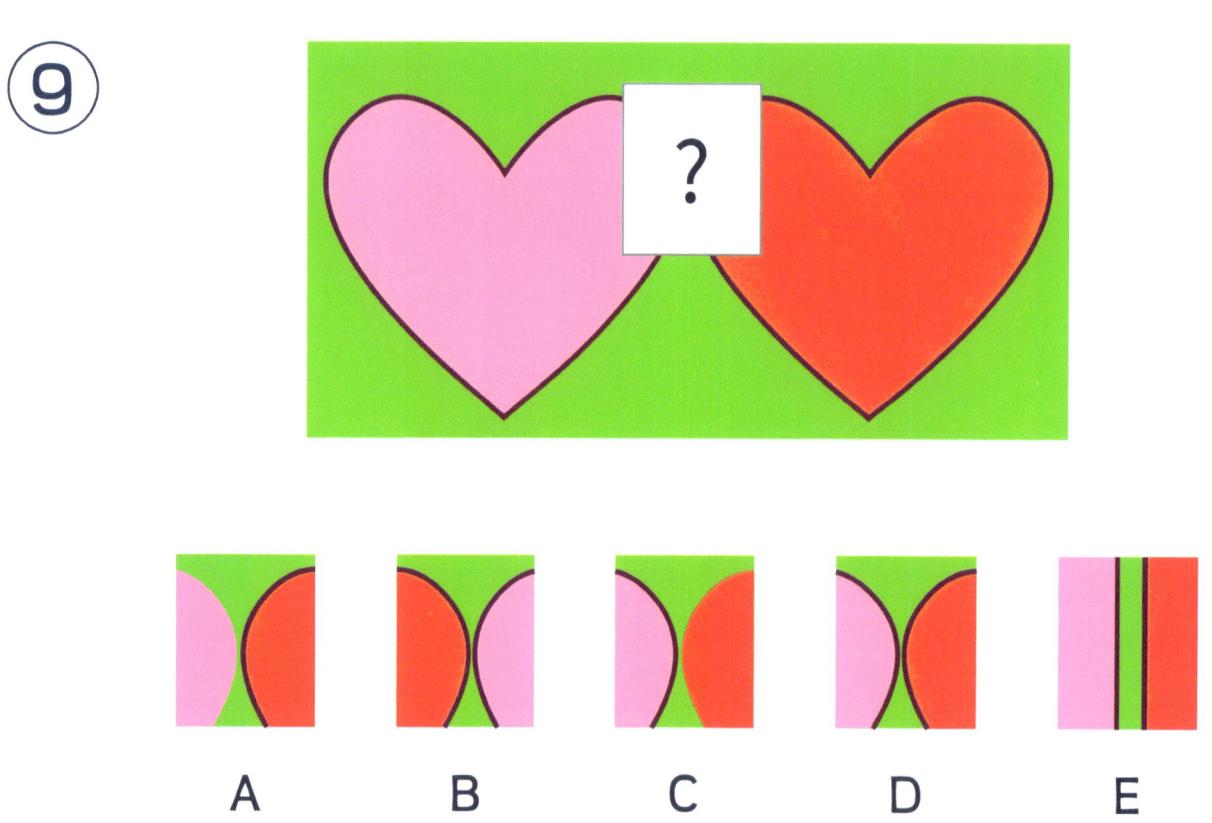

A　B　C　D　E

10

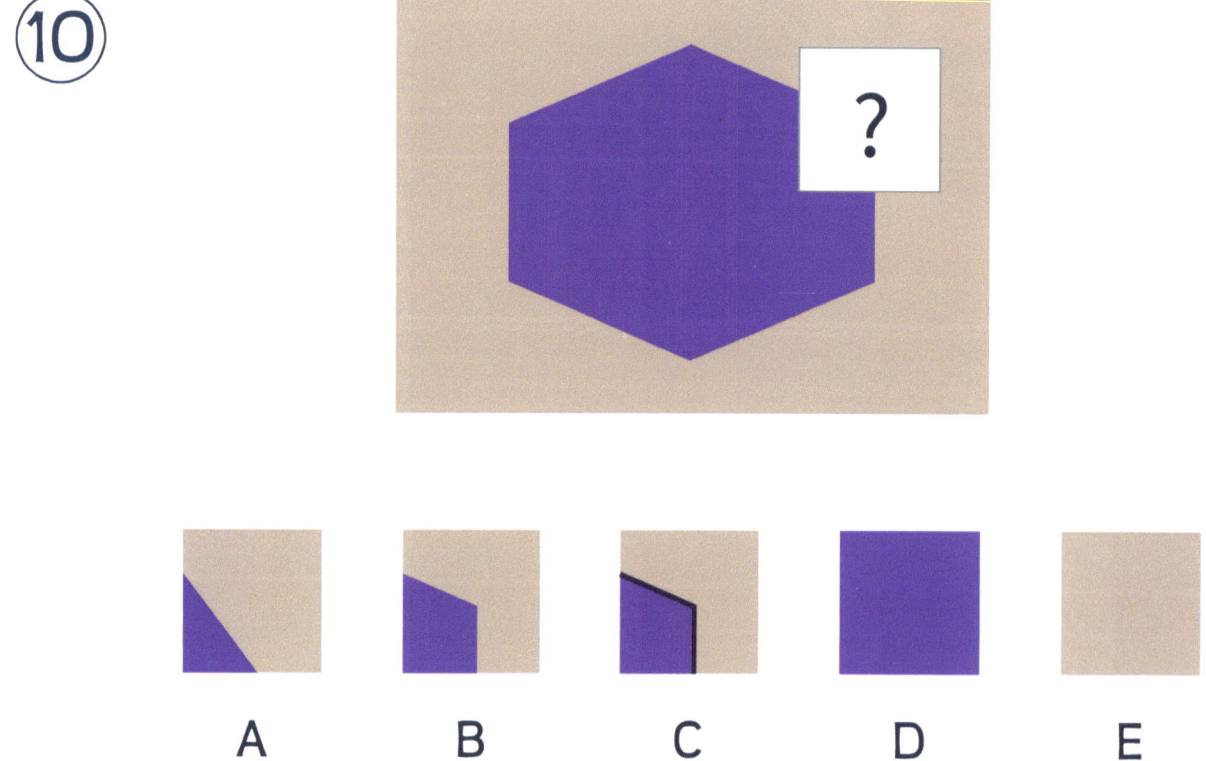

A　B　C　D　E

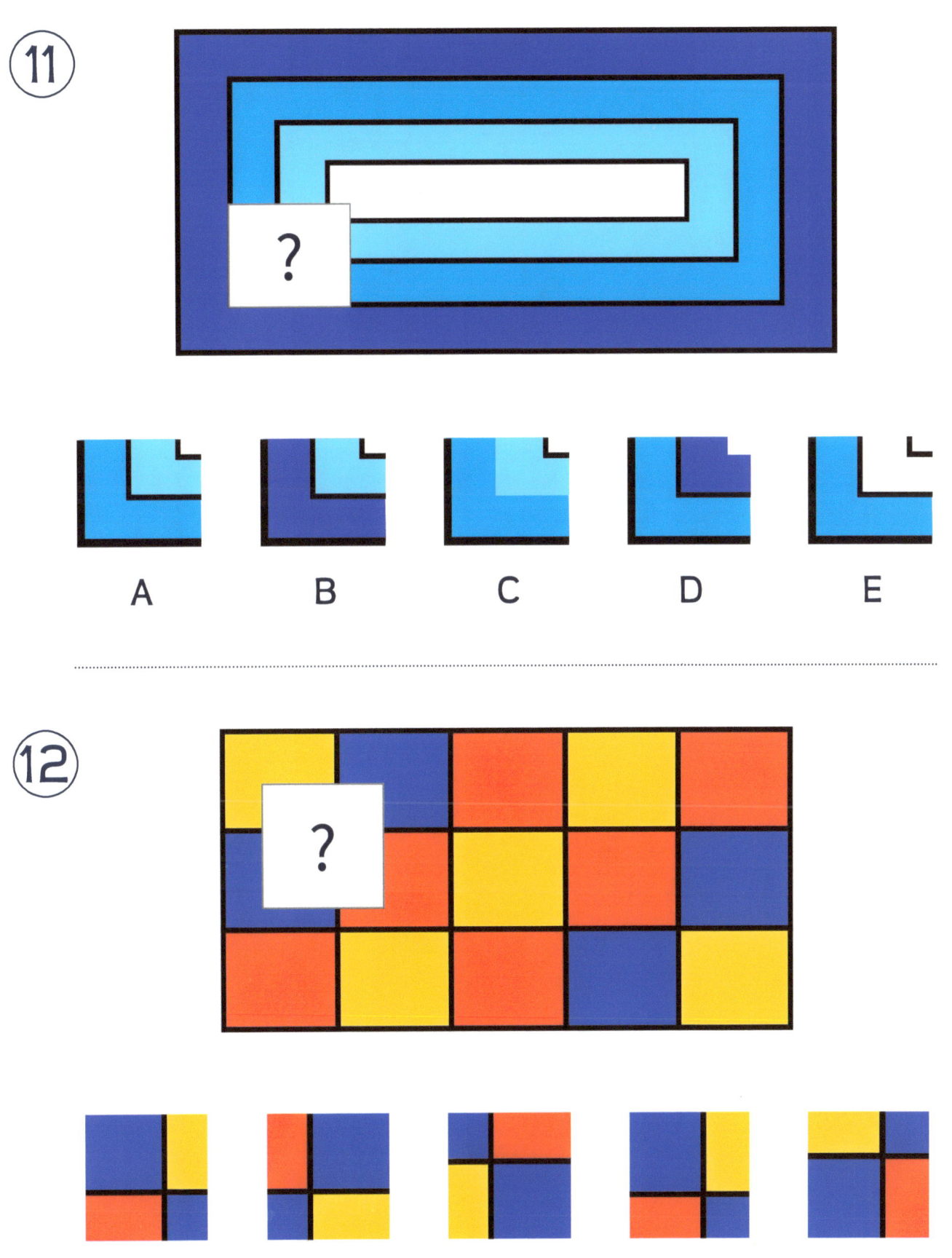

13

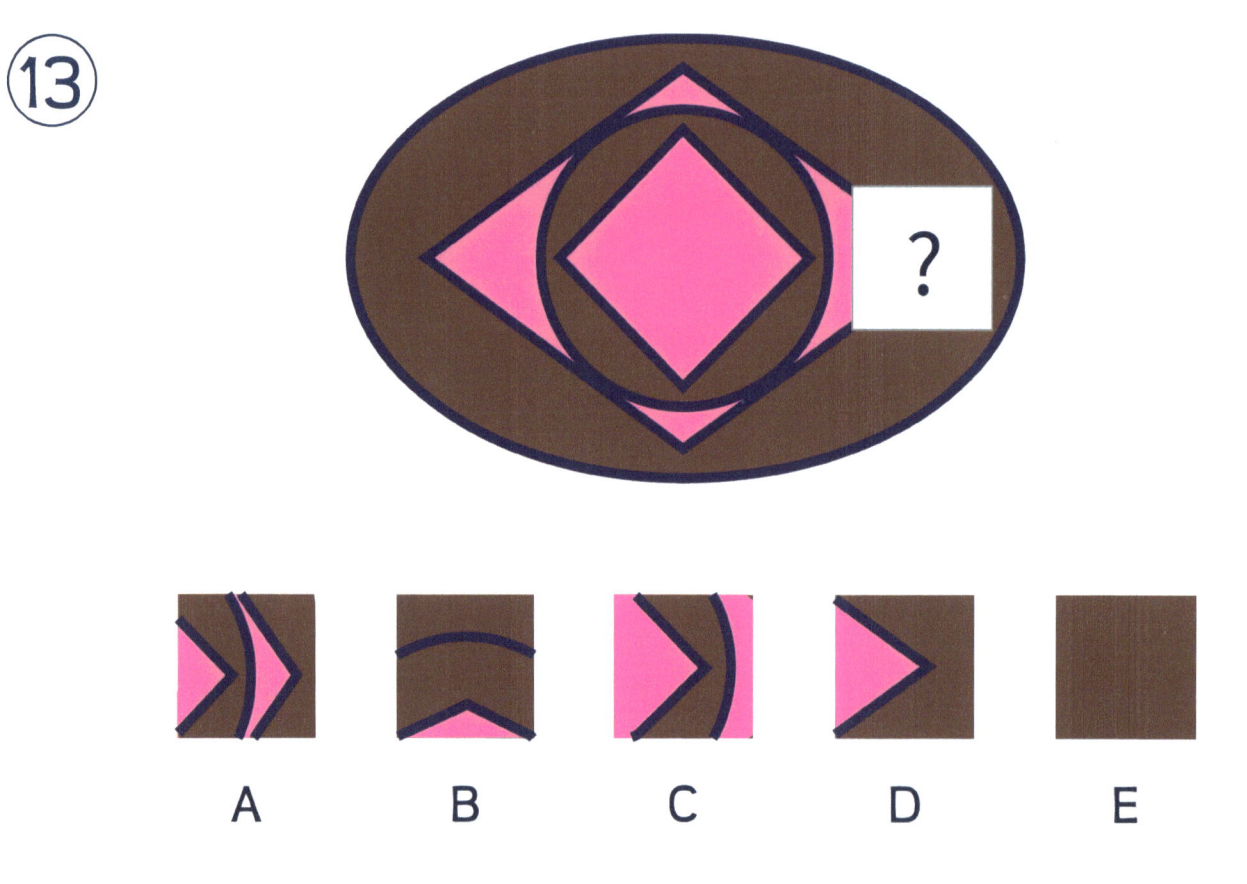

| A | B | C | D | E |

14

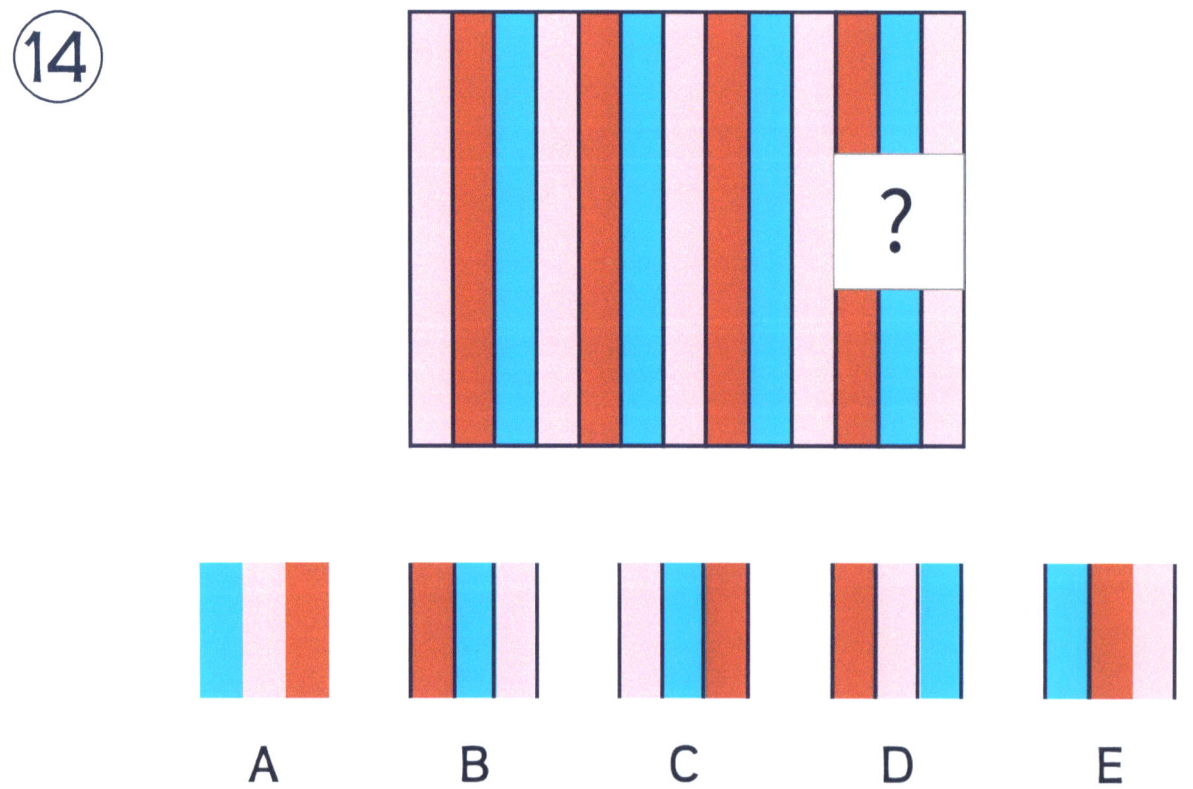

| A | B | C | D | E |

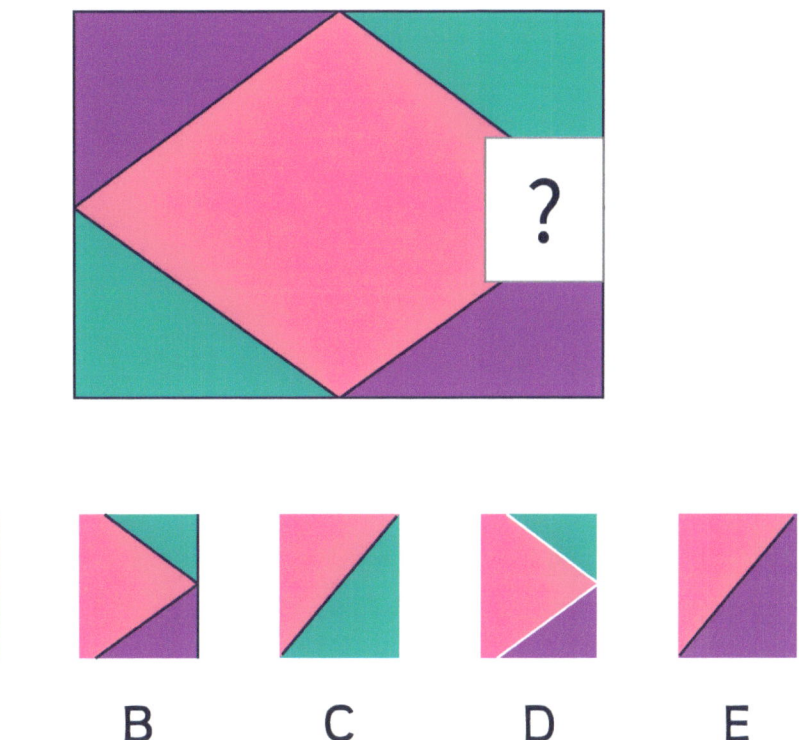

Reasoning by Analogy

These questions are analogies using geometric shapes instead of words. For each question, a reference relationship is first presented to the child, followed by a second incomplete relationship. The child must determine what the relationship is between the first set of characters and apply the relationship to the second set of character in order to answer the question correctly.

NNAT 2 - Reasoning by Analogies

1

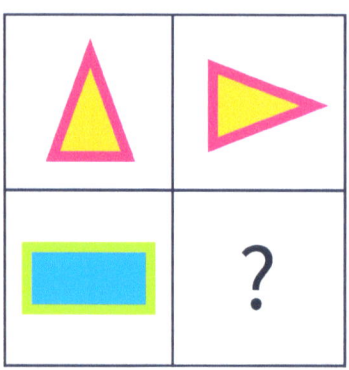

A   B   C   D   E

2

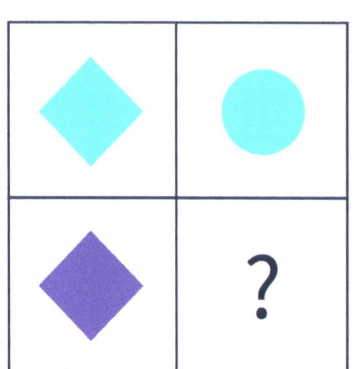

 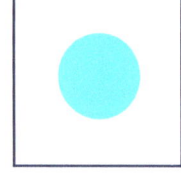 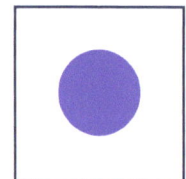 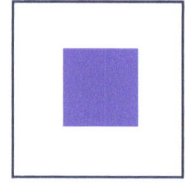 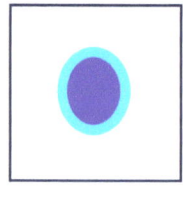

A   B   C   D   E

	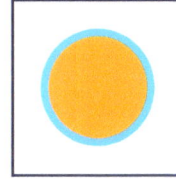			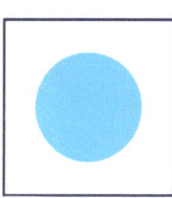
A	B	C	D	E

A	B	C	D	E

NNAT 2 - Reasoning by Analogies   Bee Tutored

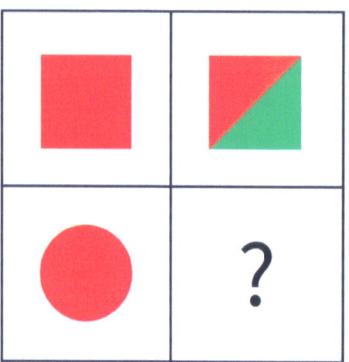

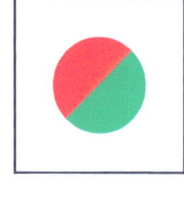   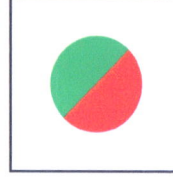      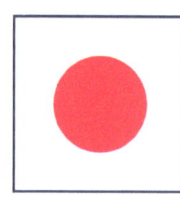   

   A   B   C   D   E

   A   B   C   D   E

A   B   C   D   E

A   B   C   D   E

⑨

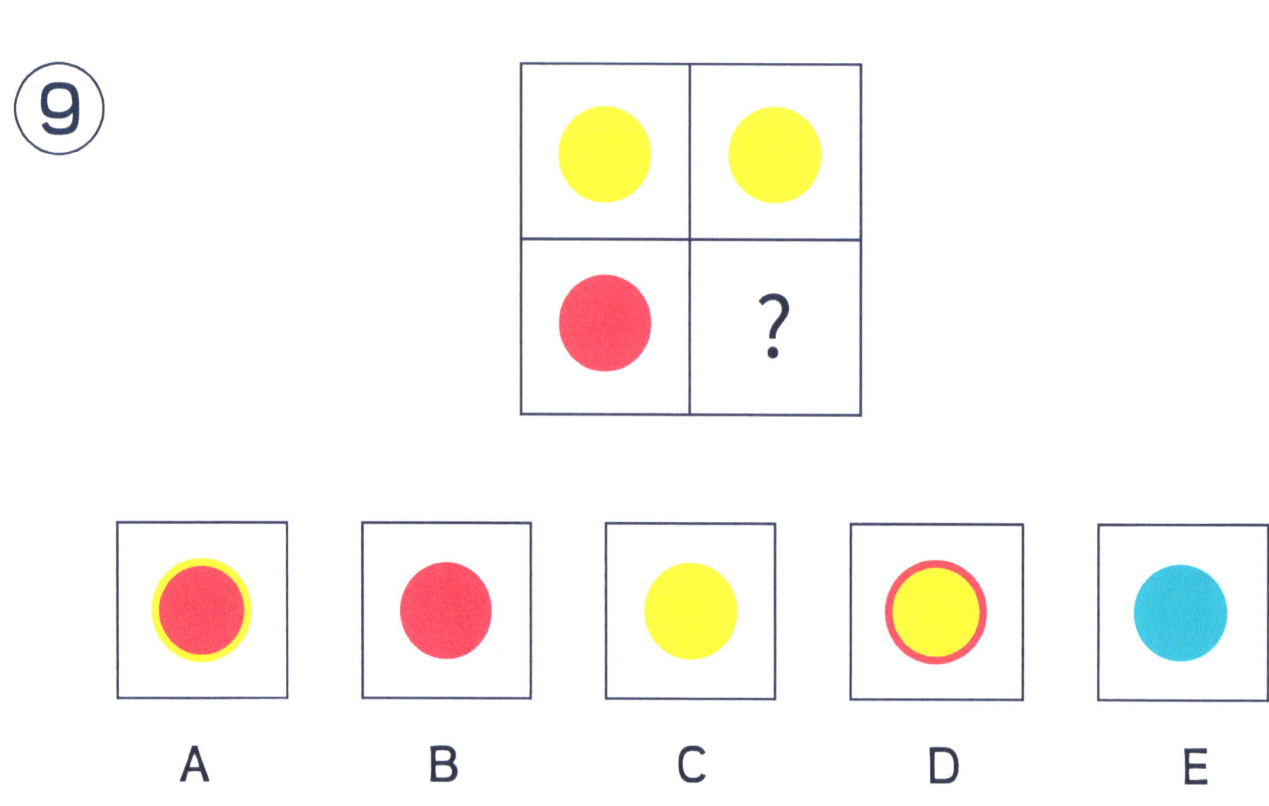

⑩

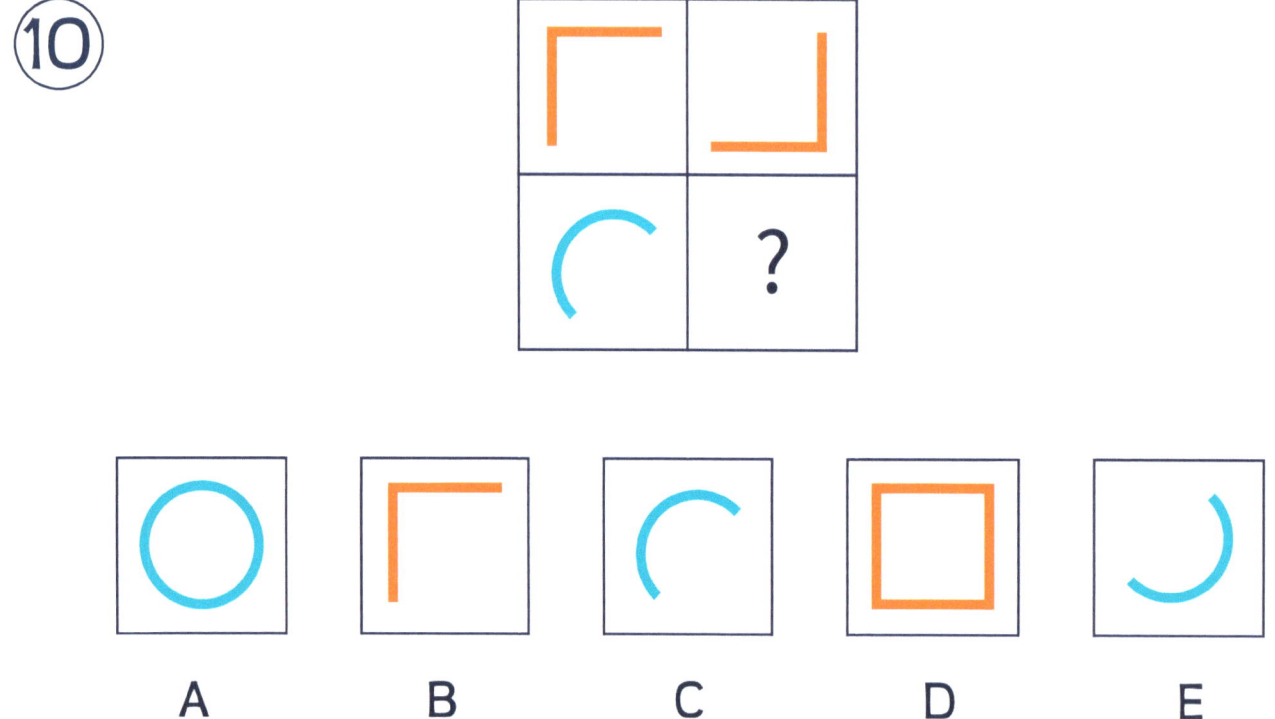

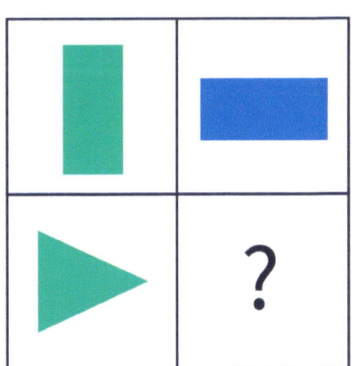

A B C D E

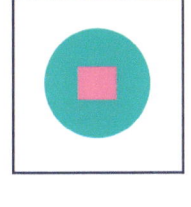    

A B C D E

NNAT 2 - Reasoning by Analogies

13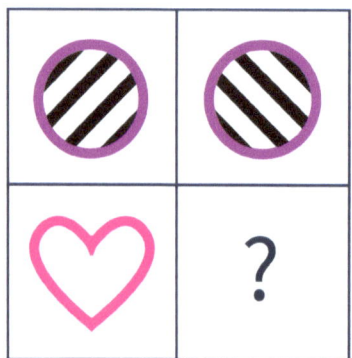

				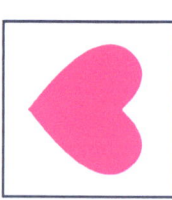
A	B	C	D	E

14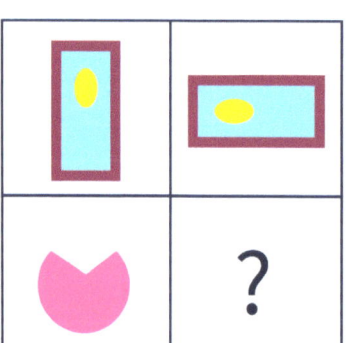

		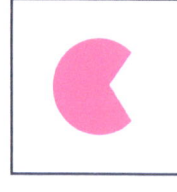		
A	B	C	D	E

 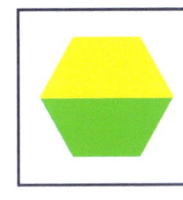 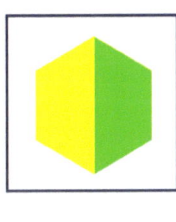  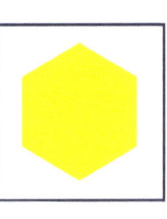

A B C D E

Serial Reasoning (Matrix Reasoning)

For these questions, the child must look at the entire block sequence, or matrix, and determine what changes in different directions. This could be color, shape, orientation, etc. Once the child has determined what "rules" govern the figure, they can then choose the missing piece. This is a more challenging type of question and is often difficult for younger children. When working with a child, the instructor encourage the student to slow down and examine how the geometric patterns change in each direction. Although serial reasoning questions are not encountered as frequently on the Level A test, children should still have practice and exposure to this type of question.

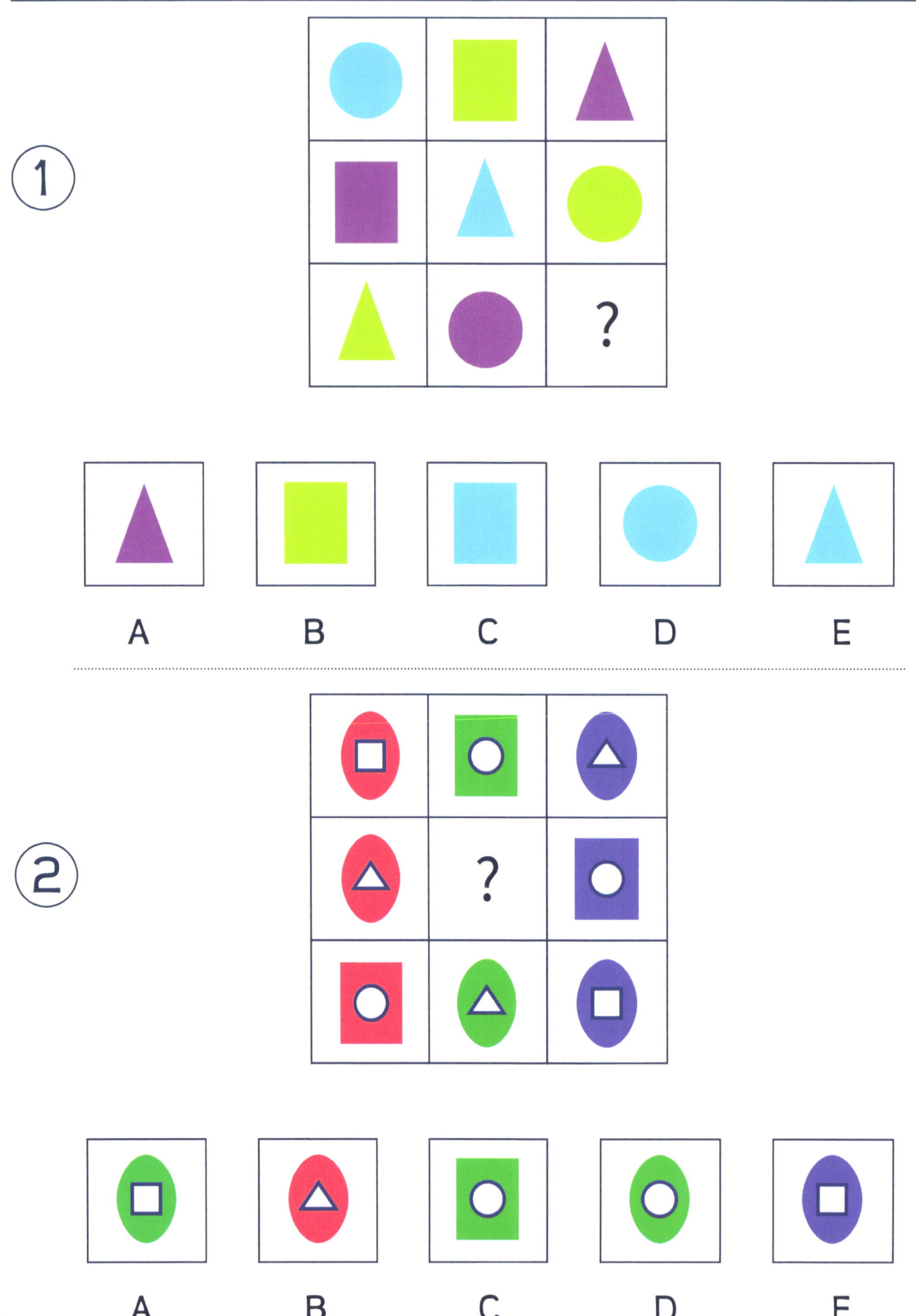

Bee Tutored NNAT 2 - Serial Reasoning

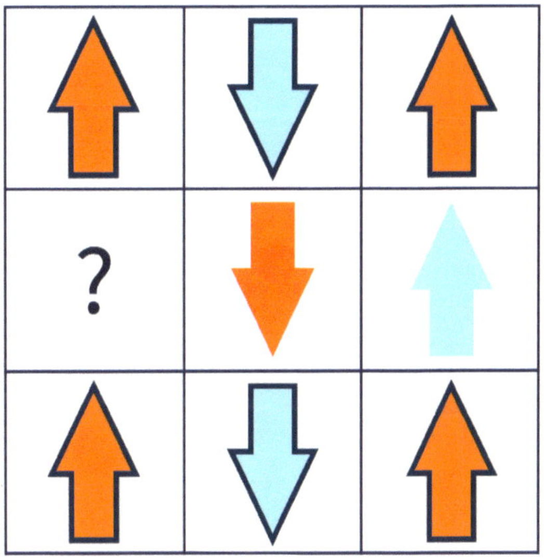

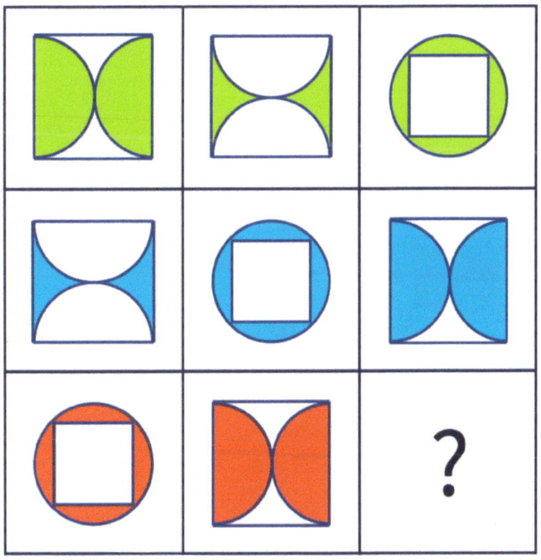

③

④

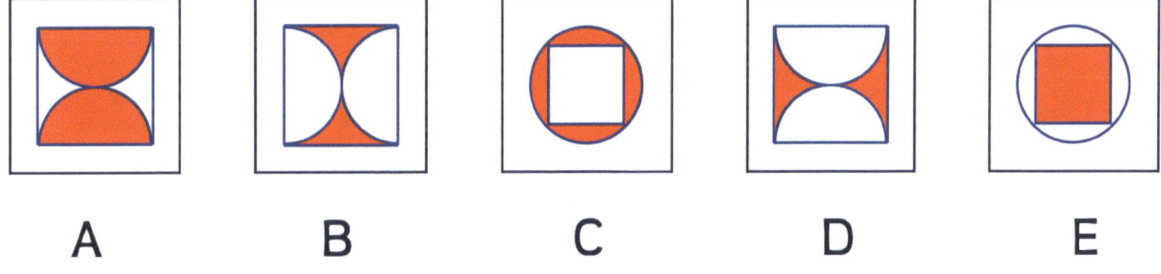

27

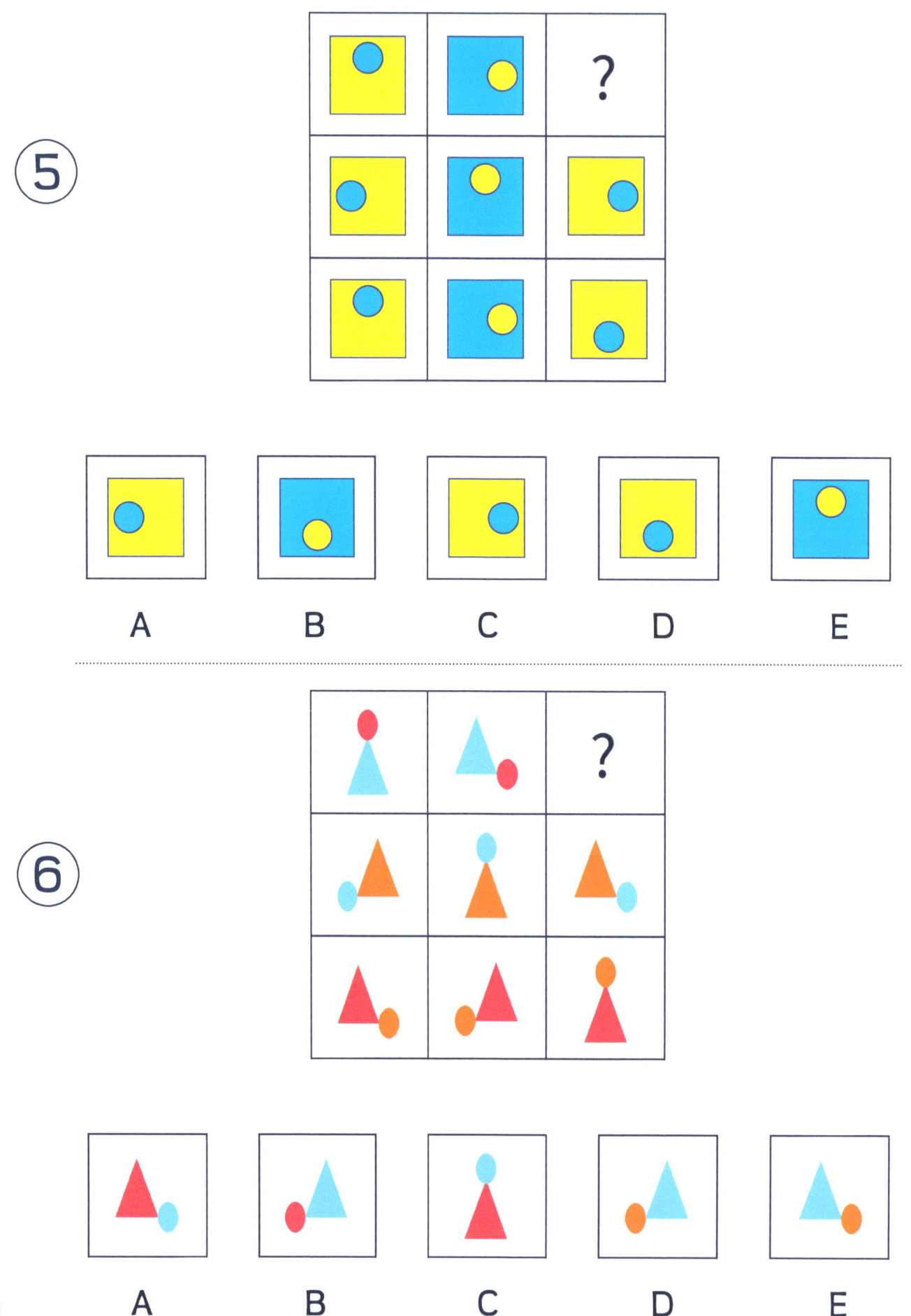

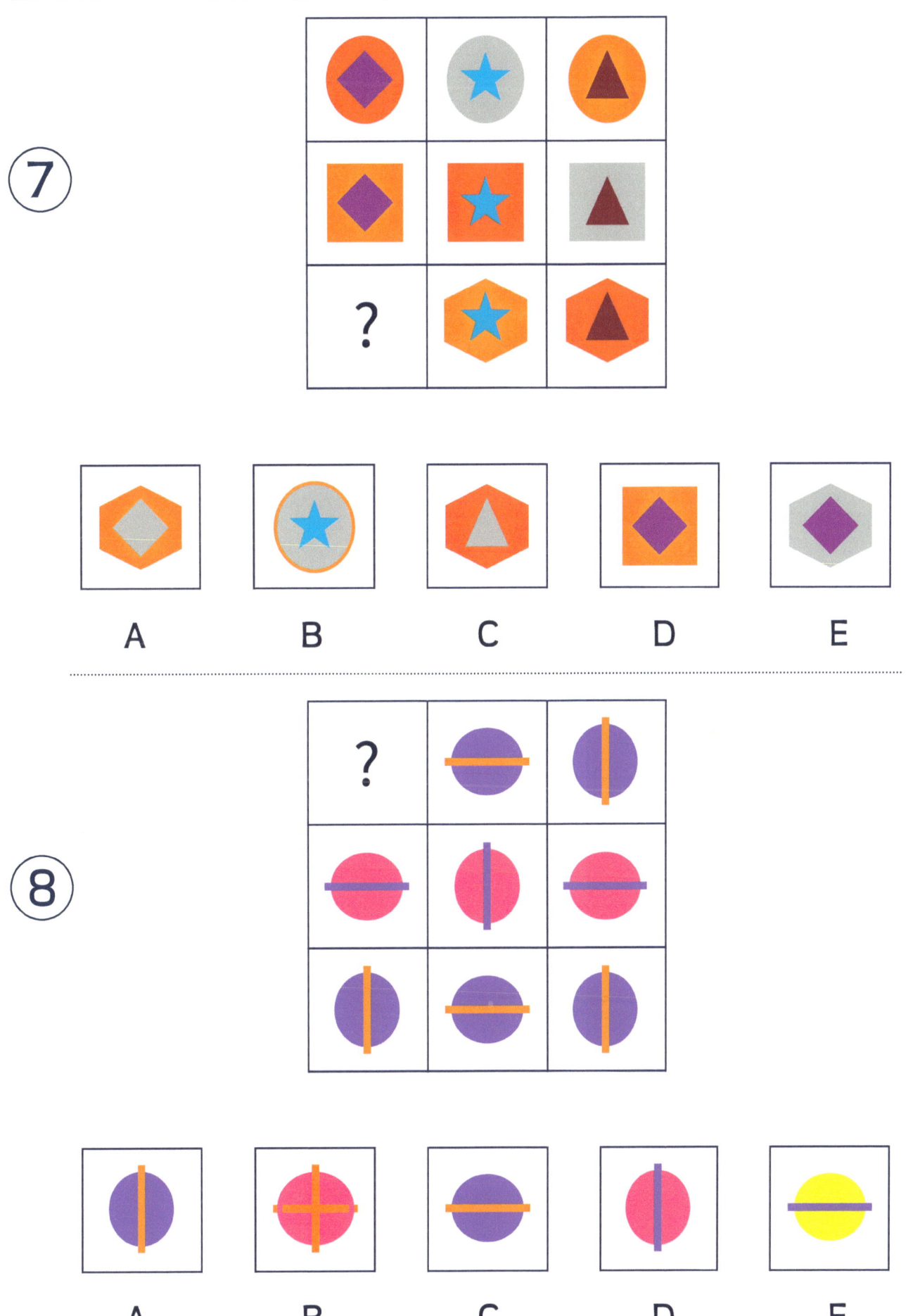

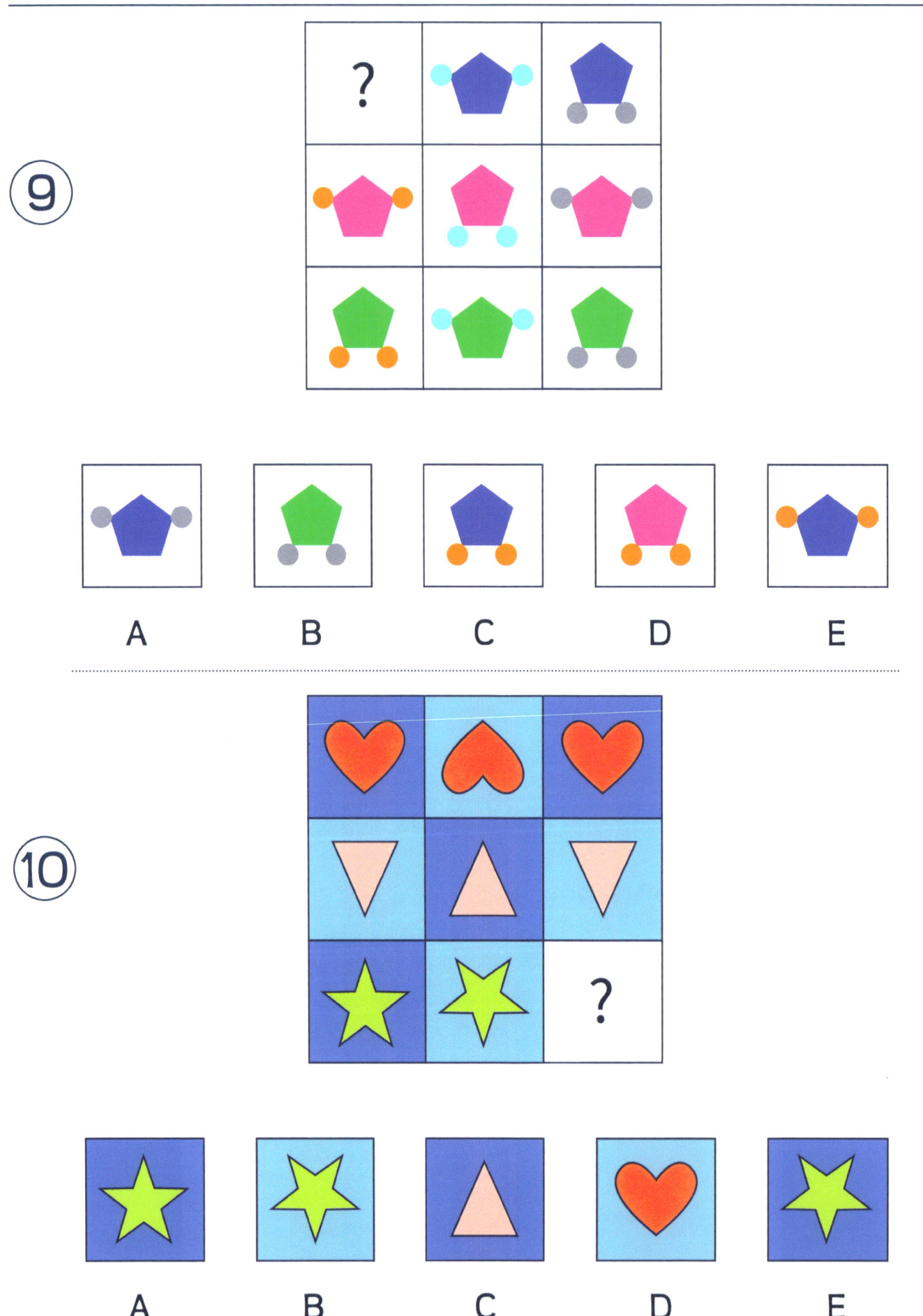

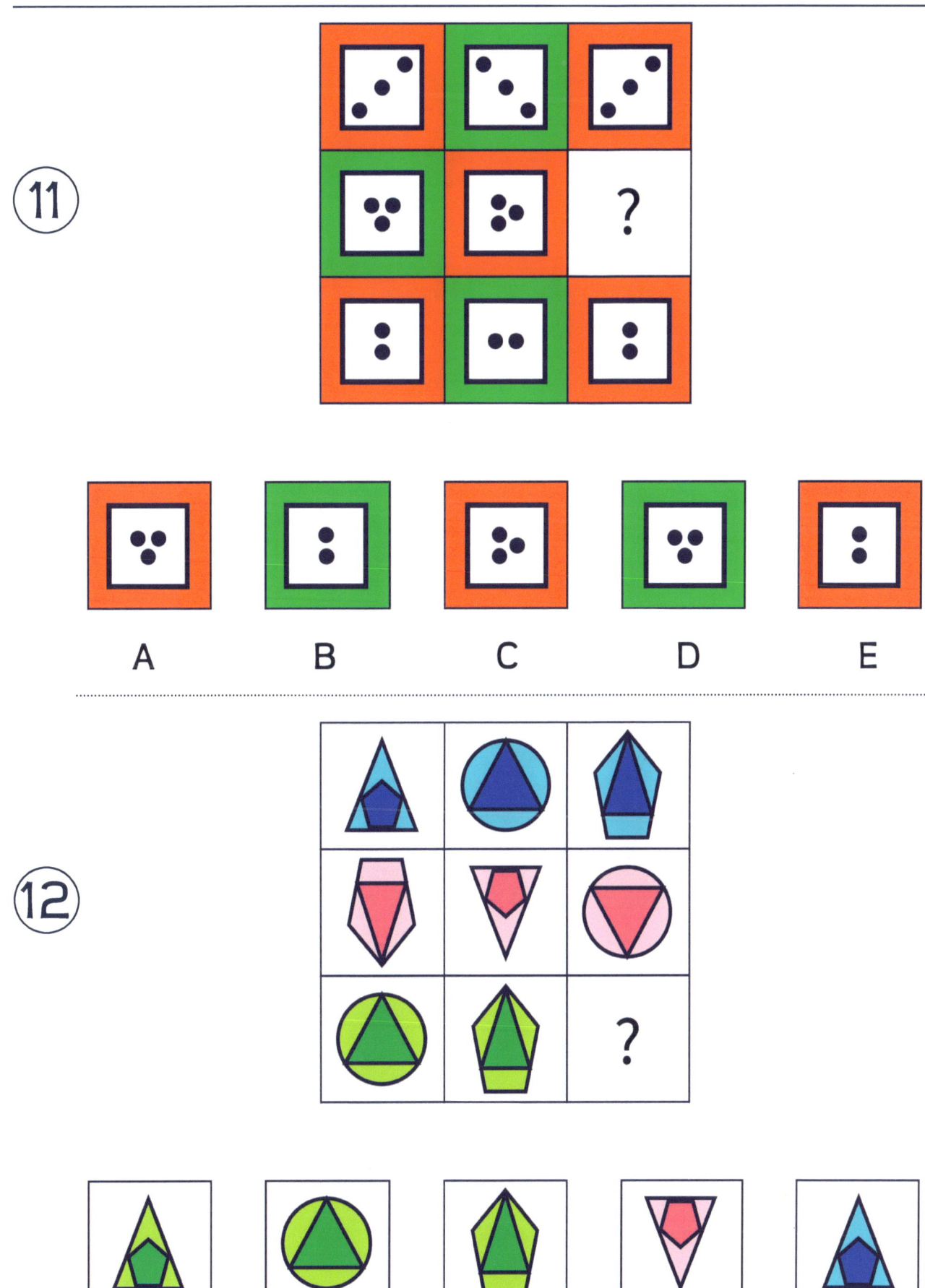

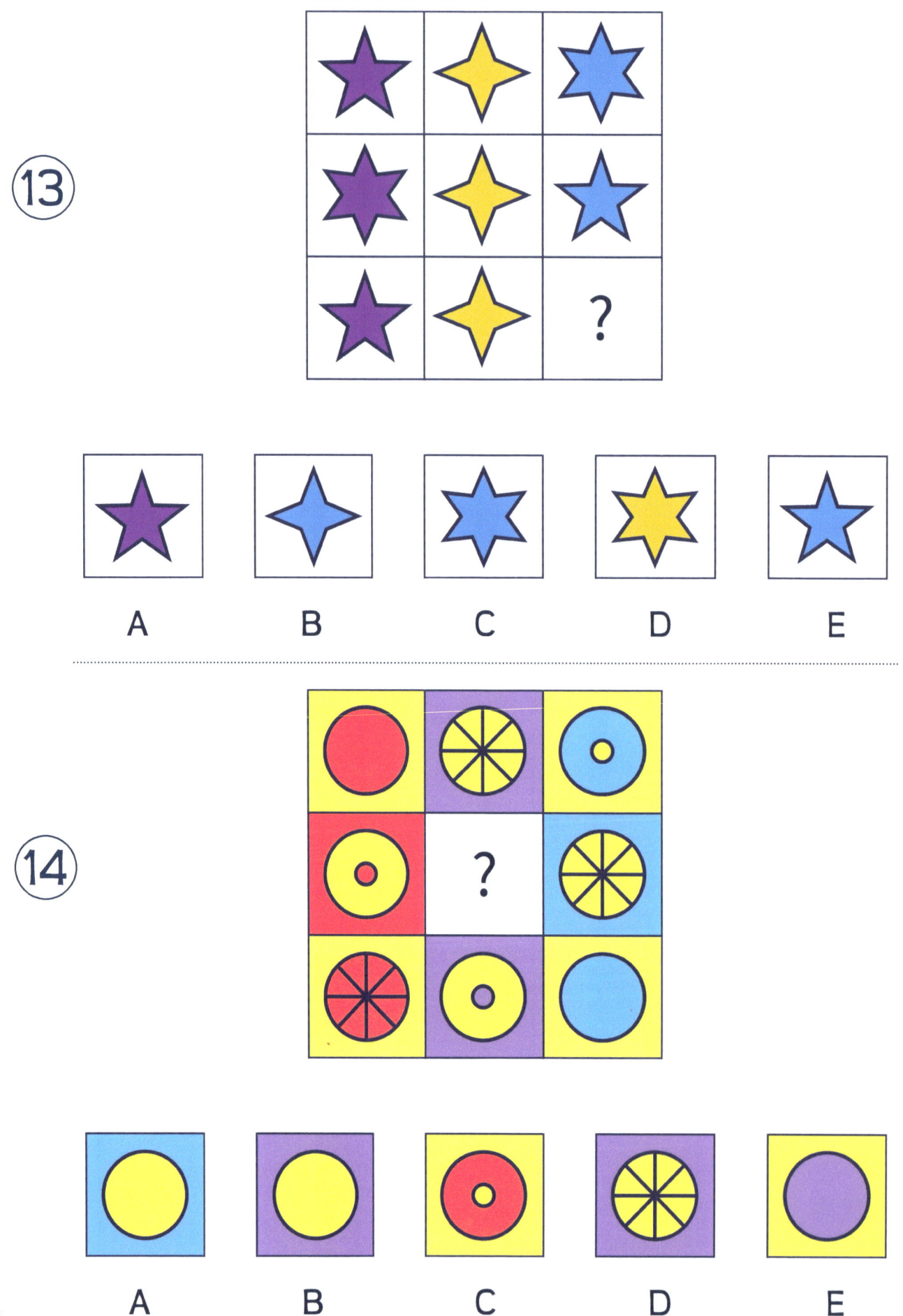

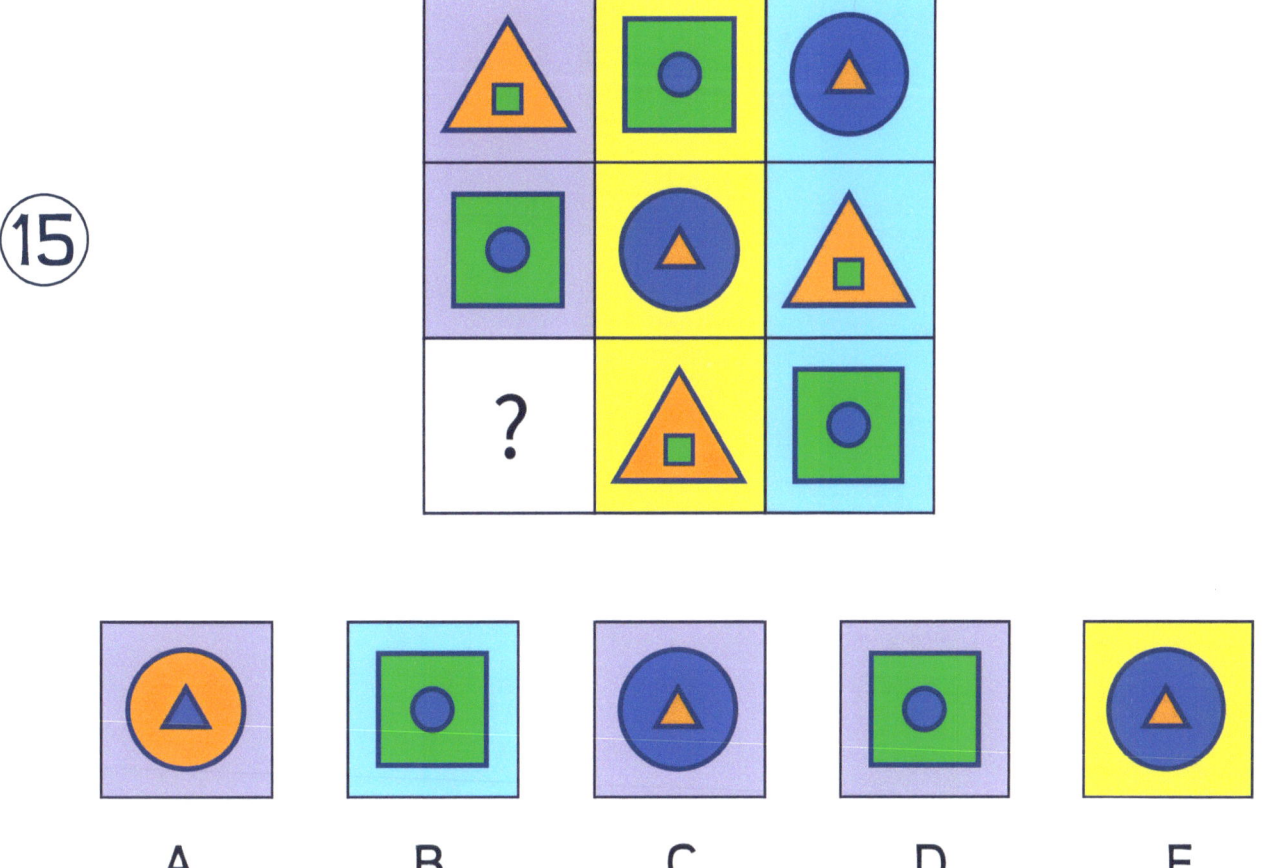

Spatial Visualization

These questions require the child to first look at two figures, often connected together, then to recognize how these figures would look folded in on themselves. The child must determine exactly how the figures are reoriented in space and apply the "rule" to the second row of figures.

For young children, spatial visualization can be visually complex because it requires the ability to manipulate figures and their spatial orientation on the mental plane. These questions are the least common on the Level A test, however exposure and practice with them is recommended.

NNAT 2 - Spatial Visualisation   Bee Tutored

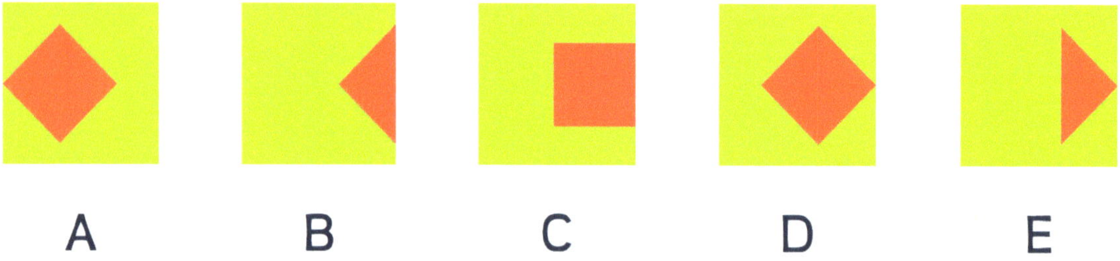

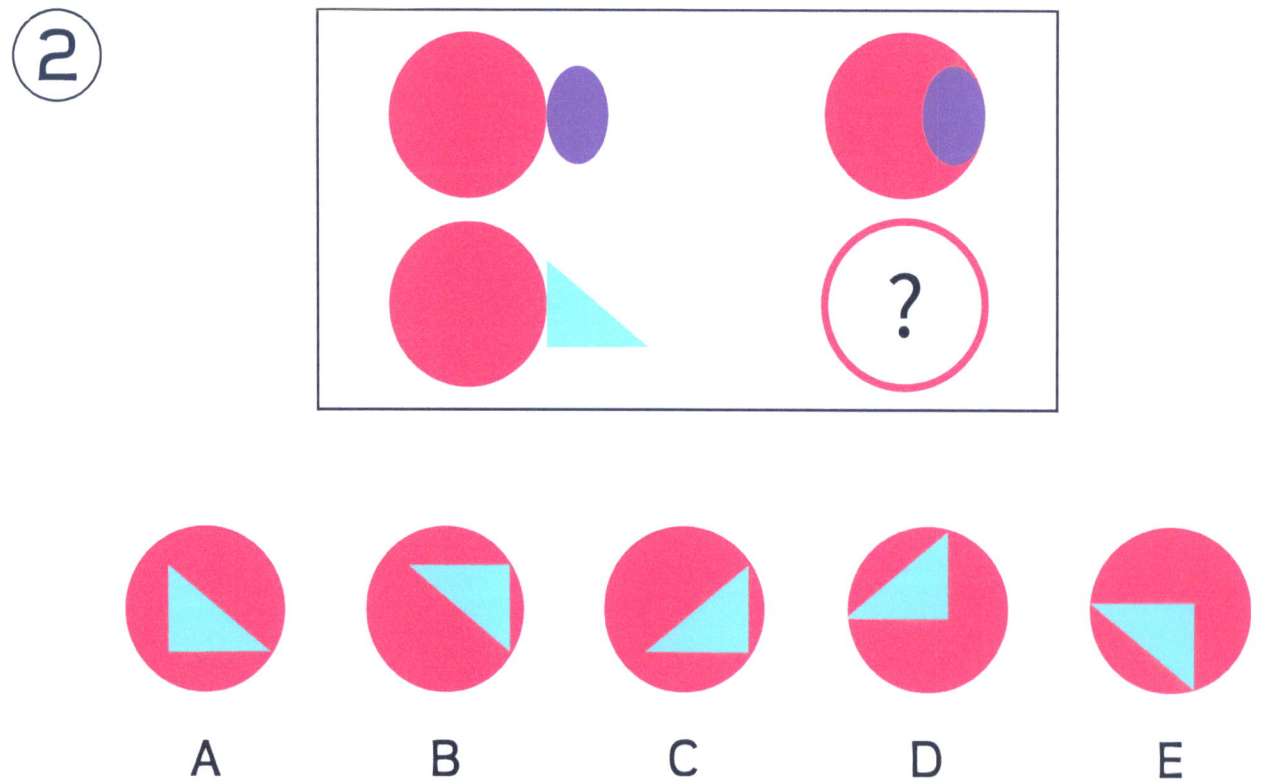

③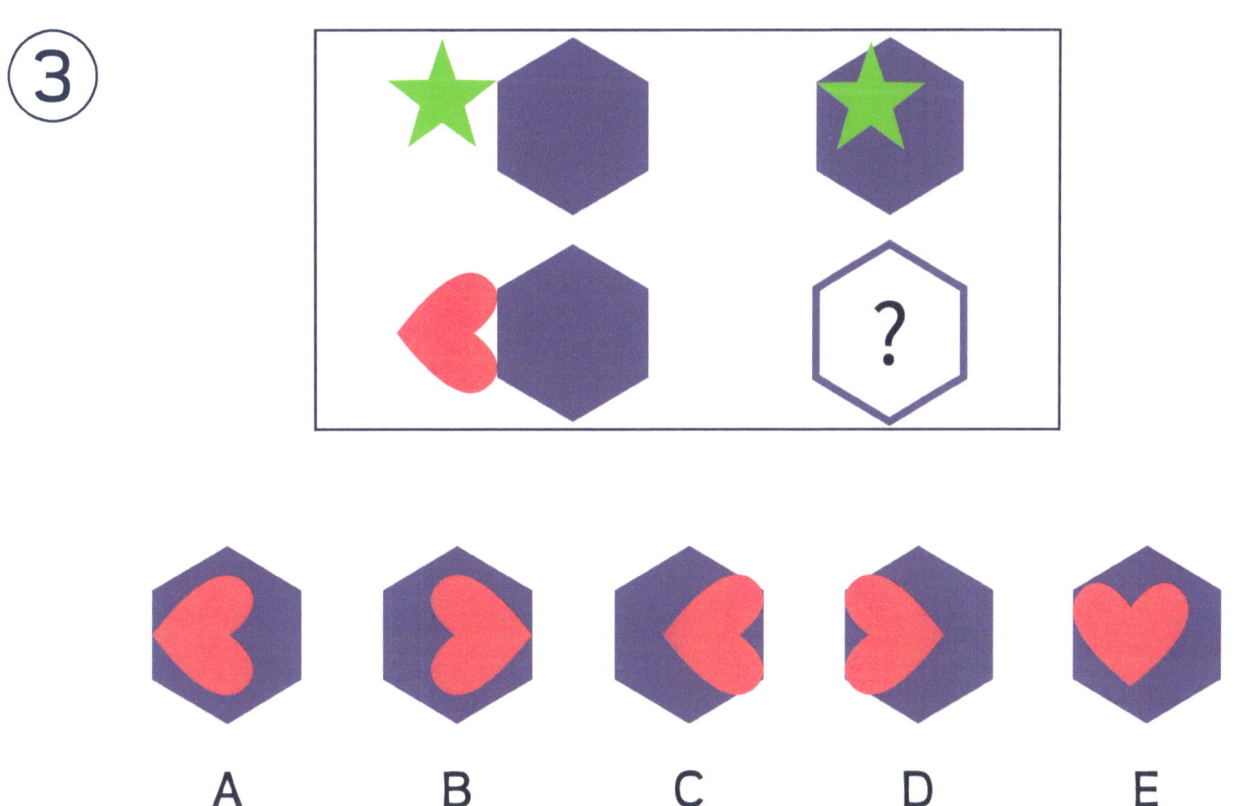

④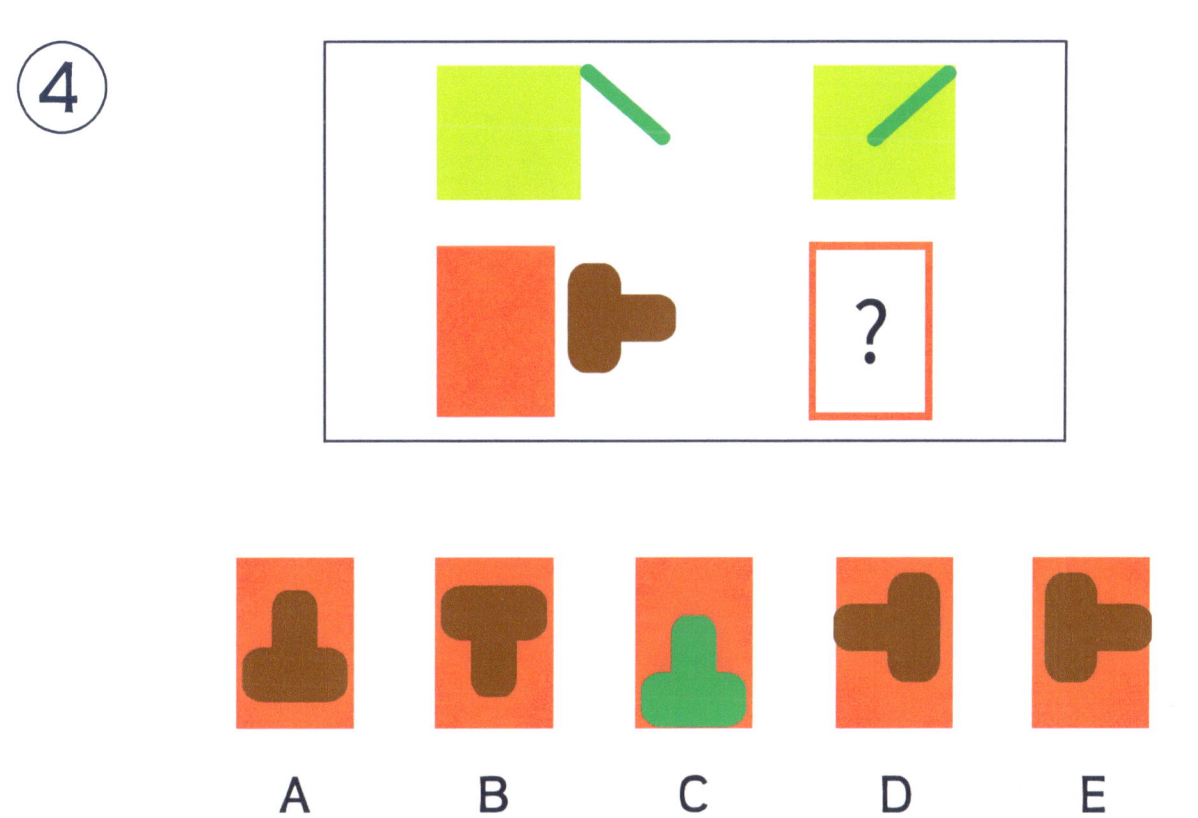

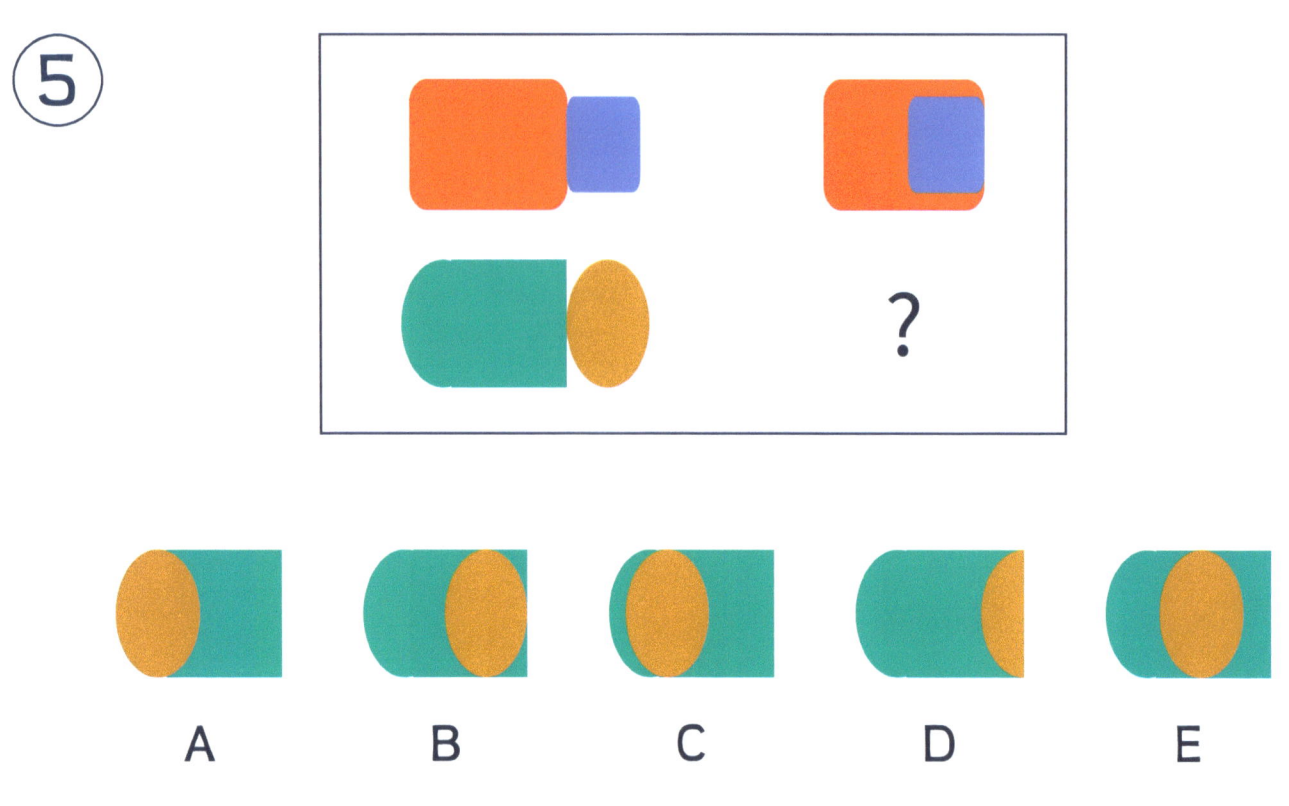
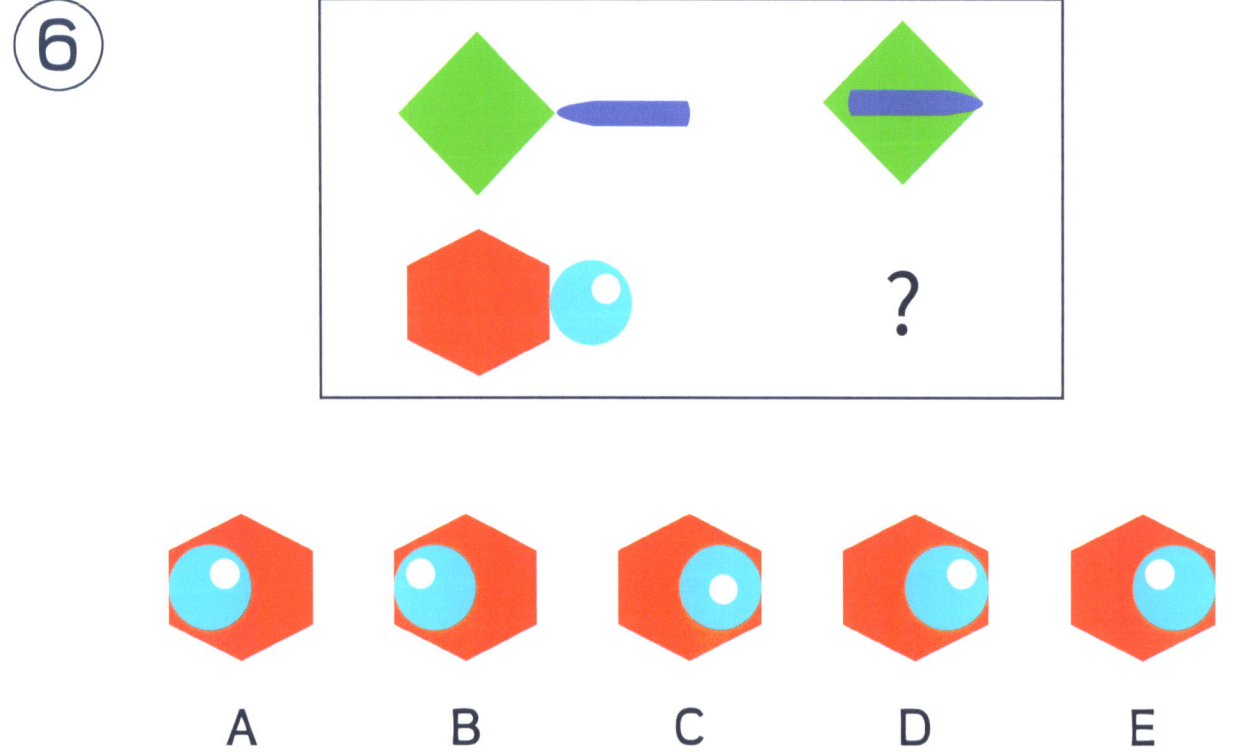

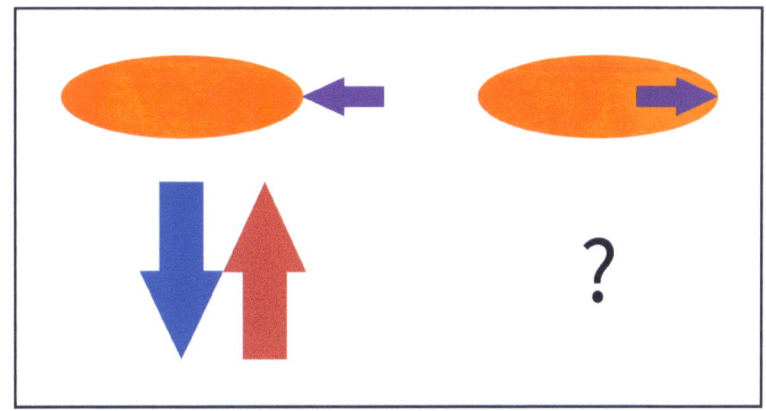

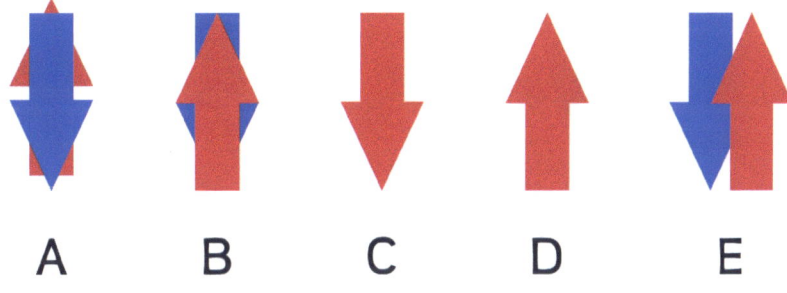

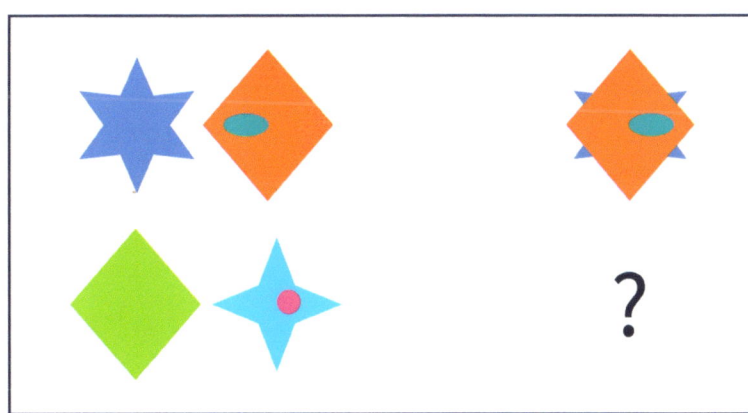

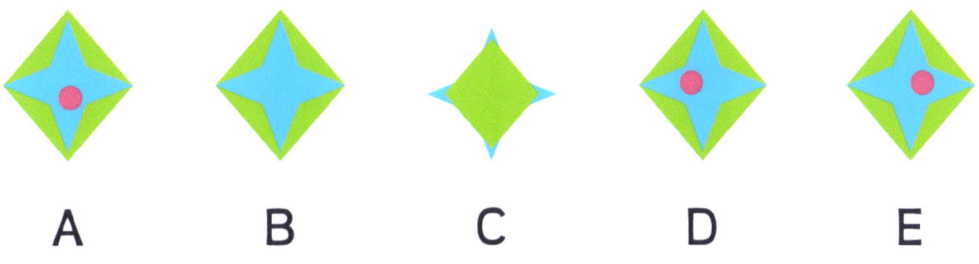

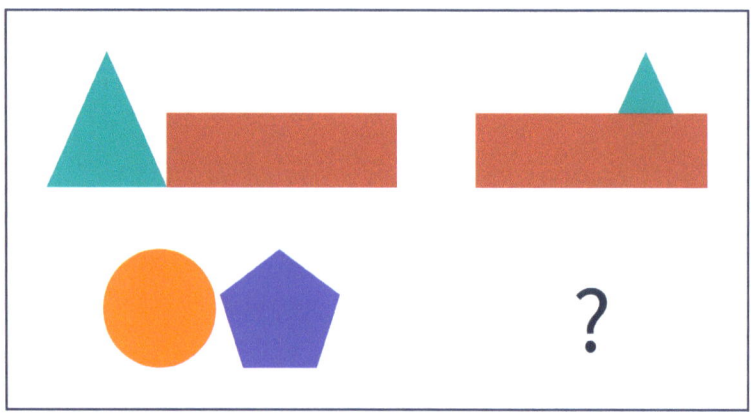
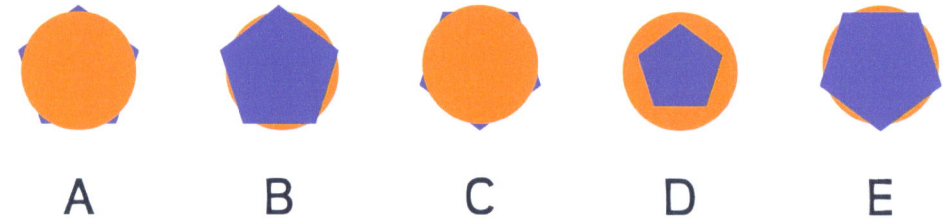

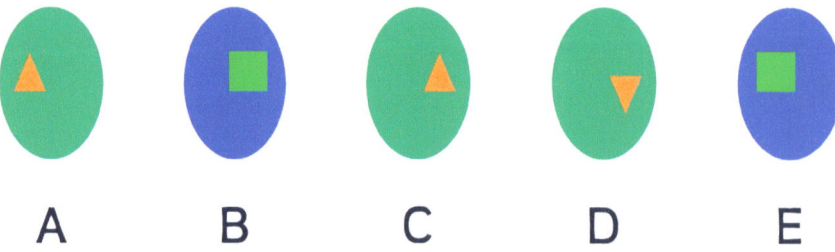

A B C D E

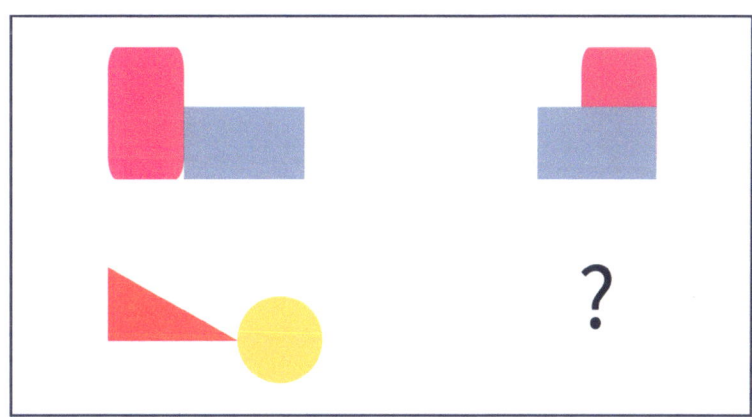

A B C D E

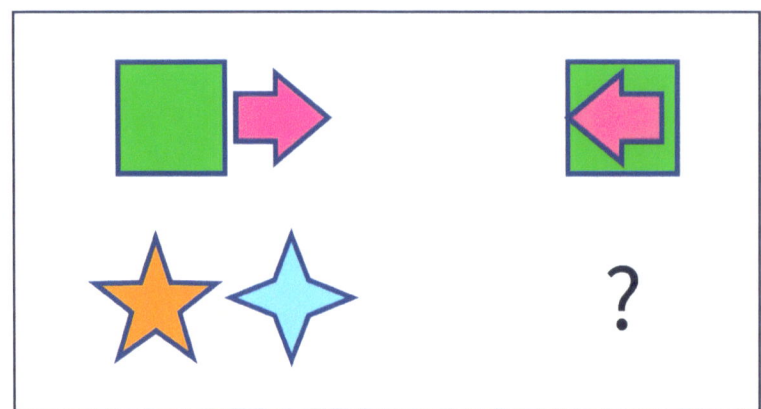

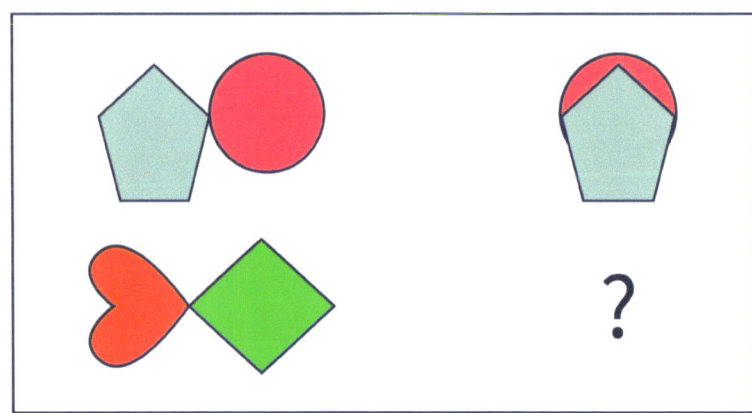
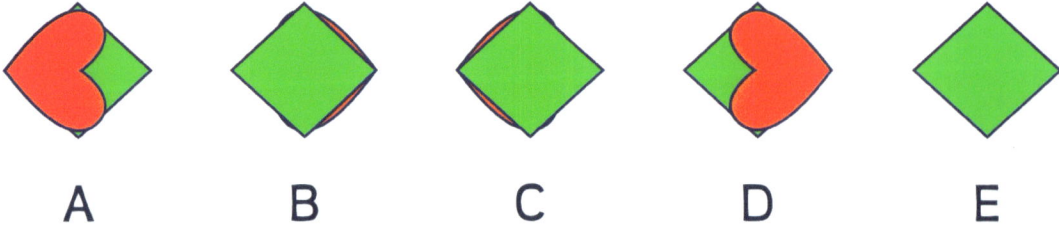

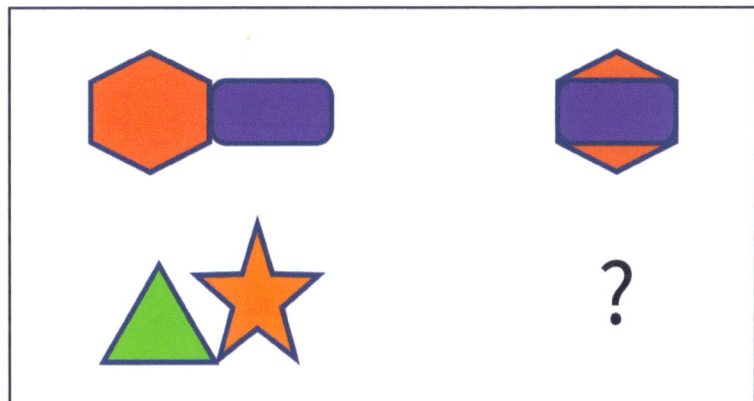

A   B   C   D   E

Answer Key

Pattern completion	Reasoning by Analogy	Serial Reasoning	Spatial Visualization
1. B	1. D	1. C	1. D
2. C	2. C	2. A	2. C
3. A	3. A	3. D	3. D
4. A	4. C	4. D	4. D
5. A	5. A	5. D	5. B
6. B	6. E	6. B	6. E
7. E	7. C	7. E	7. B
8. A	8. D	8. A	8. D
9. D	9. B	9. C	9. B
10. B	10. E	10. A	10. A
11. A	11. B	11. D	11. C
12. E	12. E	12. A	12. D
13. D	13. B	13. C	13. B
14. B	14. E	14. E	14. A
15. B	15. D	15. C	15. E